SYSTEM DESIGN INTERVIEW

System Design Interview: The Ultimate Guide to Master All the Fundamentals of System Design & to Get Ready for the Interview | Including More Than 30 Questions & Case Studies to Practice

LIAM DESANTIS

Contents

Introduction

System design is designing a system's architecture, components, and interfaces to meet end-user requirements.

It is a broad field of study in Engineering and comprises various concepts and principles that will help you design scalable systems. These concepts are widely asked in interview rounds for SDE 2 and SDE 3 positions at various technology companies. These senior roles require a well understanding of how to solve a particular design problem, respond when there is more traffic than expected on your system, design your system's database, and many more. These decisions must be made carefully with scalability, reliability, availability, and maintainability in mind. We will cover all these terminologies in this book.

Before we start discussing terminologies, there are a few things we need to clear up. When you are presented with a system design problem, you must approach it in a planned manner. Initially, the problem may seem huge, and one can easily get confused about how to start solving it. Also, there is no fixed solution while designing a system.

There are several principles you must follow to guarantee the availability of your system:

Your system should not have a sole point of failure. Your system shouldn't depend on a single service to process all your requests. Because when that service fails, your entire system can be compromised and unavailable.

Detecting the Fault and solving it at that moment.

- Scalability in system design:

To guarantee scalability, you should be able to estimate the load your system will experience. Several factors describe the load on the system:

- Number of requests that arrive in your system to be handled per day
- Number of database calls created from your system
- Number of a cache hit or miss requests to your system
- Currently active users on your system

System design is a special kind of creative design that includes in the created model all the features that, to some extent, affect the process of developing and creating an object, the conditions for its consumption, and its subsequent functioning.

System design is a universal way of organizing activities. System design is a universal way of organizing almost any type of activity. System (or software) design is based on a systematic approach used in scientific research. The principle of this approach is that understanding any object as a whole helps to see the structural elements that make up this object. An example is the university system. It includes the following elements: institute, faculty, department, specialty, and specialization.

Object as a whole. One of the fundamental principles is the understanding of any object as a single whole, including certain structural elements. This chain is almost endless.

The viability of any system depends on how functional its structure is. The successful existence of systems with an insufficient or excessive number of elements is impossible. The main requirement of a systematic approach is the following rule (principle): the structure must have the necessary and sufficient number of structural elements. Entering a single complex, the elements acquire new qualities that were not previously inherent in them, thereby generating the properties of the whole. Not a single element of the system can work in isolation, without connection with others.

Using a program-target or system approach in the design practice made it possible to consider the subject and tasks of this type of activity from a fundamentally different position.

The subject of system design is a complex design

The subject of system design is the complex design of an object, the basis of which is the phased interaction between the designer and the customer.

The personal characteristics of each of them, and the circumstances of the initial contact with the object in a communication situation, to a large extent, affect the state of the entire project. Everything matters socio-demographic characteristics, previous life experience, the degree of familiarity with the object, the ratio of the sensual and the rational in mind, the emotional state at the time of contact, etc.

The designer develops an image further implemented in the created object, investing a significant part of his personality and idea of the future design product. It depends on his professionalism to what extent the project considers the client's wishes and in what form the product will appear before the potential consumer.

As a rule, the process of direct perception takes Already in the project, and the designer lays the future unity of the object's target orientation, content, and formal qualities. This work is based on objectively existing factors that determine the general nature of design - nature, society, man, and culture.

Man is a biosocial system, the functions of which are dual. They are laid down by nature and implemented in society. Culture determines the interaction of man, society, and nature. In it, one can distinguish spiritual, artistic, and material facets. Considering all these factors, the designer develops the function (action) of the object, which serves as the basis of the design content. It (function) is expressed in the structure of visually perceived manifestations of the future object.

In the traditional concept of design as a design activity, the interaction process between a person and the design of an object was reduced to a single act - the effect of impression. Today, the process of interaction is long, and it consists of several stages of interaction.

Chapter 1: Principles of System Design

Every journey starts with Planning

If you are a product designer and are starting a new project, you might potentially find yourself in front of a blank sheet of paper with the task of drawing this map. You need to map out a route that will guide your team on their way to the perfect product. If you screw up a little at this stage, you can safely imagine yourself with your entire team moving straight toward the cliff at great speed.

What you need to create first is a clear and detailed idea of the system you are about to build. It is about system design or design system. Please do not confuse it with the design system. In theory, it sounds simple but can be incredibly difficult in practice. After all, how can you map something that doesn't even exist in reality yet?

" Systems design requires all participants to come to a common understanding before embarking on the creation process."

System design is analogous to creative cartography. This is equivalent to creating a map before creating the territory itself.

Creation of system design

Maybe I'm running into it. After all, I decided to talk about what is probably the most abstract and nebulous part of the design. I'm trying to talk about how to form conceptual ideas and successfully implement them in the brain of my colleagues. That is why many of us resist this stage of work. However, I assume it can be broken down into relatively simple elements.

In practice, the result of system design work usually results in a diagram: boxes and arrows mainly describe the core parts of the product and the way they all interact with each other. Good systems design reveals:

- Components: What are the main elements and objects in the system?
- Relationships: How are the elements connected? What are the relationships? Where are the entrances and exits located?
- Goal: What can we achieve?

Creating this map is often a process shared with the entire team while using the board. The whiteboard is the best tool: fast, easy to modify, and you can't get lost in the details. But tools like Miro are great digital alternatives. Regardless of the materials, the result is almost always the same - a clear diagram illustrating the objects and their relationships.

You may think you can avoid this hard work and talk things over quickly. But the language can be very vague: what I think and what you think can be very different, even though we may use the same words.

Moreover, most products that require the creation of such maps can rapidly become more complex as they develop. And in general, it is almost impossible to keep a clear picture of a complex system in mind.

Therefore, you need to be able to schematize your ideas accurately. Draw a map on paper. And most importantly, remember that your team must agree with what you will create.

System design alignment

Getting to this point may not be easy. Here are some common issues you may encounter:

- Subjective preferences: Often, not everyone agrees on which option is the best and worthy of implementation.
- Striving for a "perfect" system: You can get lost in system design where the goal is ideal and perfection rather than practical value.
- Different mental models: Designers naturally think in terms of composition and user experience, and developers in terms of code architecture. These points of view must converge.
- Scope Growth We often expect too much from a system and think it should solve all problems. Once people start working on a project, they see that everything is interconnected. This makes them add more and more features.

This is the whole point of systems design. Anything that makes the whole process so difficult is why it needs to be done. It's tricky because you must be clear about ambiguities, make the unknown known, understand how the system will work, and negotiate it all with each other on your team.

The goal is to catch all inconsistencies before mistakes cost you as much. You don't want to find that all your work for weeks or months has gone down the drain, and besides that, you have to pay for all the edits out of your pocket. You'd rather deal with it all from the start.

So, inevitably, you will reach the point where you realize that you have a project you quite like. You need to get all your colleagues on board and start collecting feedback.

Purpose of the principles

If you're familiar with this step, you'll already know that it often happens in Design Crit, where you provide feedback on the user interface. You make your comments using generally accepted principles.

For example, when giving feedback on the user interface, I try to formulate any feedback as objectively as possible. "I don't like how this toolbar looks" is bad feedback because it's extremely subjective. "Try to make the toolbar more like the other menu items; that would increase the consistency of the whole interface" is a much better example because here, the comment is built on the principle of consistency and is open for discussion.

This approach to providing feedback has worked well in criticizing user interface design where neither Fitts' Law nor Gestalt principles exist. The lack of clear laws is the main reason feedback can be of inadequate quality: being too subjective.

Principles of good systems design

1. Keep it as simple as possible

Do not complicate the system to solve hypothetical problems that it may encounter in the future. Try to predict future problems is great, but we shouldn't exaggerate in planning for contingencies that might not even happen.

If we can make a system more functional without adding tons of complexity to it, then that's great. But otherwise, analyze this item more carefully.

Introspection questions: Can we make the system simpler? Are we making too many assumptions about what might be needed in the future?

2. Make sure everything is clear

A good system should be simple and easy for users to understand when interacting with the product. They should be able to look at the user interface (while we are designing it) and determine what part of the system is rough. Slack is a great example.

Questions for self-reflection: Is the system's architecture obvious in the interface? Will users be able to figure it out without a further explanation?

3. Move complex elements to rarely used parts of the system

Assuming that any system bears a certain burden of functional complexity (Tesler's law), consider where it is best placed. For example, it will be much easier to schedule a meeting of the entire team to solve a specific problem once than for customer support employees to reschedule customer calls due to the lack of a solution to the problem because this will happen hundreds of times a day.

Questions for introspection: Is this system too complex initially?

Do not take on non-core problems

Don't get distracted by implementation details. Remember that when you design a system, you are not designing the entire product but its major interconnected parts. When designing a system, it is necessary to describe the form of the solution. You don't need to answer every question in detail.

Try to find out what basic tasks the system can handle and what additional tasks you can solve already when designing the user interface.

Self-assessment questions Do we need to address this section of the problem at the system level?

4. Build the system from simple to complex

One of the dangers of focusing on big clients is that you can alienate yourself and create unnecessary complications for other clients. It is too easy to design a system only for the needs of the most sensitive users. The most elegant systems allow simple use cases to scale as needed.

Intercoms, for example, are used by two-person startups that want to communicate with their customers and by huge teams to complete various tasks. You need a system that performs well for simple tasks and easily scales as needed to solve more complex tasks.

Introspection questions: Which parts of the system are relevant for all users? What parts are niche?

5. Priority is given to the existing system

Other things being equal, choose a system most similar to existing ones. First, it will be easier for you to build it. Secondly, it will be easier for users to adapt to it.

Systems design is an ongoing process, not a one-time project. Your product will evolve, and with any changes, you need to analyze the changes in the system.

Introspection questions: How difficult is it to get to the level of existing systems?

Chapter 2: System Design Interview

How to behave in an interview

It's simple - talk. Each step must be announced in advance. Don't write code before discussing it with the interviewer. The interviewer aims to understand how you think and find your strengths. If, for example, you know two solutions to a problem (say, simple and complex or effective and not very effective), then voice both and speak about the pros and cons of every single option.

Perhaps, in the first stage, this is all. Just don't forget to prepare a few questions about Facebook. I hope the first stage will go smoothly and you will receive an invitation to the second stage, which we will discuss now.

How to pass an on-site interview in the office

Unfortunately, it is difficult for me to tell you about the trip to the Facebook office since I did not have it due to COVID-19. My virtual on-site interview consisted of four calls with a break in the middle. If it were possible to choose between a virtual second stage or a real one, I would hesitate for a long time to determine which is better. In the case of a real trip, you will visit the Facebook office, stay in a cool hotel and see an interesting city at the company's expense. Still, in the case of virtual interviews, you will have the opportunity to look at your cheat sheets during a break, get a little distracted, and generally feel more comfortable at home.

The second stage will consist of four interviews with four different people: two technical interviews + behavioral + system design.

Regarding the technical part: it is identical to the one in the first stage (a couple of general questions, two tasks, and your questions). There will be only one change: the tasks will become a little more difficult. If, at the previous stage, it was worth solving problems of the easy-medium level, now it's time to switch to medium-hard (but still with a bias towards medium).

And now the most interesting. Let's talk about interviews, about which, as a rule, there is the least amount of information.

How to pass a Behavioral interview

This interview may seem the simplest, but it's not at all. Prepare carefully! Take a good look at your memory and answer the following questions about yourself:

- strengths (5-7 points);
- weaknesses (2-3 points);
- successes, especially at the last place of work (depending on the duration of work, 2 or more points should be obtained per year);
- failures (2-4 points);
- conflicts/disagreements with colleagues and managers, how did you solve these issues (it would be nice to have 2-3 examples in reserve);
- examples of proactivity, what results from it gave (4-5 points);
- your goals, how you achieve/achieved them, in which direction you want to move in the future (2-4 points);
- why you want to work on Facebook and skills that will help you realize yourself as efficiently as possible (2-5 points);
- what motivates you at work (also 2-5 points);
- examples of positive and negative feedback from colleagues and managers, how did you react to it.

Of course, you will not need all the points in the interview. Still, I highly recommend preparing a stock of answers so you can adjust to the interviewer during the interview and direct the conversation in the most comfortable direction.

An interesting feature of this interview: if you already have more than 2-3 years of experience, then be prepared to talk about the bad rather than the good. Behavior in complex, conflict, and uncertain situations will show how good you are in your soft skills.

For example, you may be asked: "What would you change at your current job?". Since there are no perfect companies, everyone has to find some answer. And, of course, this question will immediately be followed by the following: "If you don't like it, then what exactly did you do to change this situation?".

How to behave in an interview? The main thing - do not lie! If there is no answer to the question, do not try to come up with something, as subsequent questions will expose you. Don't try to present your weaknesses as strengths, but rather tell how you work to eliminate certain weaknesses.

System Design interview

So, we come to the very last and probably most difficult part. Your seniority level is assessed for this part, and your income level will depend on this assessment.

What is this interview? This is a discussion of the architecture of an application/service. Imagine that you are the CTO of a small company, and you need to come up with, draw and explain the project architect of the entire company: from junior developers to the CEO. For example, if this is an iOS position, then be prepared that the application will communicate with the cloud, asynchronously download data and media files, cache all this goodness, etc.

The most interesting question is how to prepare. For example, if you are an iOS developer, take your iPhone, look at the applications you use most often, and start drawing architecture. Ideally - ask a few colleagues/friends (of course, rummaging in your subject area) to help. Sit down together and describe the architecture of one of the applications. The more diagrams you draw, the easier it will be for you at the interview.

In real life, of course, you don't need to come up with architecture in 40 minutes, there is always a day-week-month to think about, and the result is beautiful and slender. At the interview, everything is different: you need to cover, not forget, delve into the details, and draw beautifully. The good news is that after preparation (provided that you draw at least a dozen architectures), you will have a pattern you can follow in an interview. For example, I knew from which side of the board which part of the application I would draw and how to connect with arrows. This helped a lot at the interview itself since it was my last and especially difficult (at least, fatigue and nerves affected).

The final version, it seems, turned out to be cleaner, more understandable, and simpler. So don't ignore this part; practice!

How to behave in an interview

Listen carefully to the task. Repeat out loud what you heard. Make sure you understand the task correctly.

Ask clarifying questions. The problem will be quite abstract, so there will be something to clarify. Do not make assumptions about the conditions; find out all the missing details in advance. Here is a sample list of questions for an iOS app: possible restrictions, interface, in-app purchases, geolocation, privacy, working in the background, push notifications, working offline or with poor connection, etc.

Start drawing and talking about your ideas. This is when you need to seize the initiative and be in charge for the next 30-35 minutes. This is what is expected of you!

Ensure to cover all parts of your architecture. Move from general to specific. Please say a little about each part, then go deep into one and not have time to explain the rest. Here is a list of what would be good to cover for iOS: network part and cloud (protocols, server load, API), UX, caching and database (Core Data, for example), access to system resources and data (camera, photos, contacts, files, location, etc.), content notifications and updates, analytics, testing, CPU/GPU/battery load.

Think about the future! The task will likely be simple, but it is useful if you build scalability into the architecture. For example, 100 records with some data come to you daily from the server. Think about how the application will change if there are 100 thousand of them, do not forget to immediately include this feature in the server APIs (pagination, for example). Do not be surprised, but even an iOS programmer will need to at least roughly describe the list of required server APIs.

That's all. The main thing is to be a leader, answer a few interviewer questions, and draw beautiful diagrams. With quality preparation, everything should go like clockwork.

In 1-2 weeks, you will receive a preliminary result, and if it is positive, then in another week, you will be sent an offer. How to voice the refusal, I honestly do not know. At Google and Amazon, this is a standard "thank you, we're impressed, but not" letter. On Facebook, positive feedback was given over the phone and very detailed, so negative feedback, I think, can be given more detail so that you know what to work on in the future.

Passing an interview is a skill. So practice, practice, and practice again. Everything is possible!

Chapter 3: Common System Design Concepts

Designers aim to produce a model or representation of an entity that will be built later. There are two important phases in any design process: diversification and convergence. Diversification is the acquisition of a repertoire of alternatives of primitive design material: components, component solutions, and knowledge, all within catalogs, textbooks, and in mind. During convergence, the designer chooses and combines the appropriate elements drawn from this repertoire to satisfy the design objectives in the same way as stated in the requirements document and in the way agreed with the client.

Concept

Architecture design defines the relationship between the major elements of the software structure, the architecture design styles and patterns that can be used to meet the requirements defined by the system, and the constraints that affect how it is implemented. The architecture.

Software design should always begin with data analysis, as it is the foundation for all other design elements. Once the foundation is obtained, the architecture is obtained. Only then should further design work be carried out.

Concepts Related To Architectural Design

- Data design: the data objects and relationships defined in the entity-relationship diagram and the detailed data content of the data dictionary form the basis for the data design.
- Architectural design is obtained from the analysis model and the interaction of subsystems.
- Interface design is the one that describes the way the software communicates with itself, the systems that operate with it, and the operators that use it.
- Procedural design is obtained from the process specification, control specification, and state transition diagram.

Design Components

- Graphic symbols identify and describe a system's components and their relationships.

- Data dictionaries: describes all data used in the system can be manual or automated.
- Descriptions of processes and procedures: technical description to describe the activities carried out by the processes.
- Rules: steps to follow to describe and document correctly and completely.

Tools

- Data flow diagram: it is the basis for other components and describes how data navigate between processes and related elements.
- Data dictionary: contains the characteristics of the fields and a detailed description of the different objects that make up the system
- Entity relationship diagram (der): describes the relationship between entities and objects (set of information contained in entities)

The Design Process

Software design is an iterative process by which requirements are translated "into a blueprint" to build software. At first, the blueprint illustrates a holistic view of software. That is, the design is characterized by a high level of abstraction, in which the specific objective of the system and the more detailed requirements of data, operation, and behavior are directly traced. As design iterations occur, subsequent improvements lead to lower levels of abstraction. These can also be traced back to the requirements, but the connection is more useful.

Software architecture design considers two levels of the design pyramid shown in the figure: data design and architectural design.

Data design makes it easy for us to represent the data components of the architecture.

The architectural design represents software components' structure, properties, and interactions.

Software Design is a sequence of steps, and it is not a recipe because they intervene:

- Creativity, experience, and a commitment to quality.
- There are internal and external quality factors.

- External. Properties that users can observe.
- Internal. The Software Engineer wants them.

The design model is equivalent to an architect's plans for a house. Start by rendering the totality of everything to be built (for example, a three-dimensional rendering of the house) and slowly refine what will guide building each detail (for example, the plumbing layout). Similarly, the design model created for software provides several different views of computer software.

According to Alan Davis, the design principles are as follows:

1. Alternative approaches must be taken in the process.
2. Shall be traced back to analysis.
3. It must be reused.
4. Try to mimic the problem domain.
5. Uniformity and integration.
6. It should be structured to admit changes.
7. You must anticipate adaptation to unusual circumstances.
8. Do not code.
9. Assess yourself for quality while you're growing.
10. Minimize misconceptions.

Software Design Model

When designing the interface, 4 different models come into play:

1. Design model created by the software engineer.
2. User model: which can be created by the software engineer or other engineers.
3. User perception.
4. Image of the system created by those who implement the system.

These 4 models can be reconciled, and a consistent representation of the interface derived, for which the profiles of age, gender, physical abilities, education, cultural or ethnic background, motivation, goals, and personality must be known. In addition, the following user categories can be established:

Beginners do not have syntactic or semantic knowledge of the application use.

Occasional and knowledgeable users have reasonable semantic knowledge but low retention of the information necessary to use the interface.

Frequent and knowledgeable users: possess sufficient syntactic and semantic knowledge, seek abbreviated modes of interaction

Design Elements

To develop the interface design, the following tools will be used:

1. Menu map
2. Design each one of the screens of the system according to the hierarchical diagram.
3. Function Point Count

Different architectural models can be produced during the design process.

Each model presents different perspectives of architecture:

- Structural static model showing the main components of the system.
- A dynamic model of the process showing the process structure of the system.
- Interface model that defines the interfaces of the subsystems.
- Relationship models such as a data flow model.

Modular Design

The software is classified into separately named and addressed components, often called modules, that are integrated to satisfy the requirements of the problem. It's easier to solve a composite problem when broken down into manageable pieces.

A module is typically a component of a subsystem that provides one or more services to other modules. In turn, it uses the services provided by other modules. Modules are typically made up of several simpler system components.

It involves dividing software into separately named and addressed components called modules, which are integrated to solve the requirements of the problem.

According to G. Meyers, "modularity is the only attribute of software that allows you to manage a program intellectually."

Monolithic software (a large program made up of a single module) cannot be easily understood by the reader.

Two main strategies can be used when decomposing a subsystem into modules:

1.   Object-oriented decomposition, a system is dissolved into a set of communicating objects. This criterion is the most used today and consists of dividing the main Problem into modules (Objects) that encapsulate the definition of the object and all its operations. It refers to small modules that will carry out an independent and specific task aimed at solving the main problem but without depending on another module; due to this, it is very easy to modify the modules without affecting others.

2.   Flow-oriented decomposition of functions, in which a system is decomposed into functional modules that accept data and transform it into output data. This criterion is the least used today and refers to dividing the main program into subprograms that group similar functions; Therefore, these modules are not independent; it is very difficult to modify them since modifying any of the modules implies modifying all the other modules.

Software Architecture And Design Of Transactional And Transformational Data

What Is Architecture?

Bass, Clements, and Kazman define this term as "the structure or structures of the system, comprising the software components, their visible external properties, and the relationships among them."

It is the representation that enables the software engineer to:

- Analyze the effectiveness of the design to achieve the requirements set.
- Considering architectural alternatives when making design changes is relatively easy.
- Reduce the risks associated with building the software.

In architectural design, a software component can be as simple as a program module. Still, it can also be as complicated as including a database and middleware that allow the configuration of a network of clients and servers.

There is a difference between the terms architecture and design. A layout is an instance of architecture, similar to an object, that is an instance of a class. For example, consider the client/server architecture. This architecture makes it possible to design a network-based software system in many ways, using a Java (Java EE) or Microsoft (.NET framework) platform. So there is architecture, but many designs can be created based on it. Therefore it is not valid to mix the terms design and architecture.

Why Is Architecture Important?

- They facilitate communication between all parties interested in developing a computer-based system.
- It highlights early design decisions that will profoundly impact all software engineering work.
- It constitutes a relatively small and intellectually understandable model of how the system is organized and its components work together.

In a broad sense, we could agree that Software Architecture is the highest level design of the structure of a system, program, or application and is responsible for the following:

- Define the main modules
- Define the responsibilities that each of these modules will have
- Define the interaction that will exist between these modules:
- Control and data flow
- Information sequencing
- Interaction and communication protocols
- hardware location

Transaction Flow

The movement of data characterizes the transaction flow through an arrival path that converts information from the outside world into a transaction. The transaction is evaluated, and according to its value, the flow follows one of many paths of action.

The center of the information flow from which the action paths emanate is called the Transaction Center. The information flow through an action path may have transformation flow characteristics within a transaction flow.

Transformation Flow

In a system, information enters and exits in a form from the outside world (keyboard entries, telephone tones, display images). These external data must be converted to a suitable form for processing.

Information enters the system through paths that transform external data into an internal form and is identified as Incoming Flow.

Inside the software, a transition occurs; the incoming data passes through a transformation center, now moving toward the software's output. These data form the Outflow.

The overall data flow occurs sequentially and follows one or a few direct paths. When a part of the DFD has these characteristics, we say it is a Transformation Flow.

Transformation Analysis is a strategy, not an algorithm. If the steps of an algorithm are followed, the results are assured and correct, and a strategy achieves good results but not perfect in a first approximation.

The transformation analysis is a set of steps that allow obtaining the system's structure from a DFD with transformation characteristics.

The DFD with transformation characteristics is one in which three zones can be distinguished:

1. Arrival or entry flow.
2. Transformation flow or transformation center.
3. Outflow.

Steps Of The Transformation Analysis

1. Isolate the transformation center.
2. Perform the first level of factorization of the Table Structure Diagram.
3. Elaborate on the second level of factorization
4. Refine the structure of the system using measures and design guides.

Transformation Design Steps

The steps begin with a reassessment of the work done during the requirements analysis and then evolve into the software architecture design. The transition from the DFD to a program structure is done in 7 steps:

1. Review the fundamental model of the system: review the DFD level 0 and the complementary information.
2. Review and refine software DFDs: Level 1, 2, and 3 DFDs are examined to the level where each transformation has high cohesion (i.e., each transformation performs a single, distinct function) and can be implemented as a module. This step reaches the level that contains enough detail to establish an initial design for the program structure.
3. Determine if the DFD has transformation or transaction characteristics: In general, the information flow of a system can always be represented as a transformation. It should be treated as such if it has an obvious transaction characteristic. The designer selects the general flow characteristic based on the prevailing nature of the DFD. Local regions of transformation or transaction flow are isolated, allowing us to refine the program's structure later.
4. Isolate the transformation center by specifying the incoming and outgoing flows: limits. The designer must set reasonable limits.
5. Perform the first-level decomposition: The program structure represents a top-down distribution of control. The decomposition results in a program structure in which higher-level modules make execution decisions and lower-level modules perform most of the input, processing, and output work. Intermediate-level modules perform some control and perform moderate amounts of work.

At the top of the program structure is a control module, which serves to coordinate the subordinate control functions, which are:

a) Incoming information processing controller, which coordinates the reception of all incoming data.
b) Controller of the transformation center, which supervises all operations on the data in its internal form.
c) Controller of outgoing information processing, which coordinates the production of outgoing information.

Each control module has a name that indicates the function of the subordinate modules it controls.

6. Perform second-level decomposition: it is done by converting the individual transformations (bubbles) of a DFD into the modules corresponding to the structure of the program. Starting within the confines of the transformation center and moving out through the input and output paths, the transformations become subordinate levels of the control structure.

Thus we obtain an initial program structure, also called a Structure Diagram.

Although we have made a one-to-one correspondence between the DFD bubbles and the software modules, you can combine 2 or 3 bubbles, representing them as a single module, or you can split a bubble into two or more modules.

Although the modules that make up the program structure have a name that indicates the function it performs, a brief text must be written for each of them that explains its processing.

The information it will contain is:

- The information that enters and the one that leaves the module.
- The information is retained in the module (for example: in data stores).
- Explanation of the Procedure, indicating the main decision points and the tasks.
- Treatment of restrictions and special characteristics, if any.

Refinements are governed by common sense and practical considerations.

7. Refine the initial structure of the program using heuristics to improve the quality of the software. The initial structure of the program can always be refined by applying the design fundamentals. Therefore, the number of modules can be increased or reduced to obtain a decomposition with good cohesion, minimal coupling, and an easy structure to implement, test, and maintain.

There are times when the incoming/outgoing data flow controller is unnecessary, input processing is required in a module subordinate to the transformation controller, or loose coupling cannot be achieved due to the need to work with global data.

The seven points above aim to develop a general representation of software. Once the structure has been defined, we can evaluate and refine the software architecture by looking at it as a whole.

Transaction Analysis

Transaction analysis is applied when a DFD takes a form in which a piece of data determines the choice of one or more information flows.

The transaction is evaluated based on its value, and the flow is initiated down one of many action paths.

The center of information flow from which various paths of action emanate is called the transaction center.

Transaction analysis steps:

Steps to follow:

1. Review the fundamental model of the system.
2. Review and refine DFDs.
3. Determine if the DFD has transformation or transaction characteristics.
4. Identify the transaction center and flow characteristics of each action path.
5. The center of the action is easily located in the DFD, and it is the origin of several information paths that flow radially from it. The incoming path and all action paths must also be isolated.
6. Transform the DFD into a software structure suitable for transaction processing.

The transaction flow becomes a program structure containing inbound and dispatch branches.

- The incoming branch is obtained the same way as the transformation analysis; from the transaction center, the bubbles are converted into modules.
- The dispatch branch has a dispatcher module that controls all subordinate action modules.
- The flow of each action path of the DFD will be converted into a structure that corresponds
- with the characteristics of the flow (transformation or transaction).

1. Break down and refine the transaction structure and the structure of each path of action. Each DFD action path has its non-transaction information flow characteristics. The substructure of each path of action is obtained by following the steps of the corresponding analysis.
2. Refine the initial structure of the software using design heuristics to improve quality. Equal to the previous.

User Interface Design

The user interface design creates efficient communication between humans and computers. Following a set of interface design principles, the designer identifies interface objects and actions and then creates a screen that forms the basis of the user interface prototype.

What are the steps?

User interface design begins with identifying the requirements of the user, the task, and the environment. Once the user tasks have been identified, user scenarios are created and analyzed, and a set of interface objects and actions are defined. This forms the basis for creating a screen template that illustrates the graphic design and placement of icons, the definition of descriptive text, the specification and titles of windows, and the specification of major and minor aspects of the menu. With the use of tools, the prototype is made, the design model is ultimately implemented, and the quality of the result is evaluated.

A house plan (its architectural design) isn't complete without representations of doors, windows, and utility hookups for water, electricity, and telephone (not to mention cable TV). The "doors, windows, and service connections" of computer software are what constitute user interface design

The interface design focuses on three areas of interest:

(1) the design of the interface between the components of the software;
(2) the design of the interfaces between the software and the other non-human producers and consumers of information (that is, other external entities) and
(3) the design of the interface between man (that is, the user) and the computer

User Interface Design Rules

There are three golden rules for interface design:

1. Leave control to the user

Most of the restrictions and limitations imposed by the designer are intended to simplify the interaction mode. But for whom? In many cases, the designer may introduce limitations and restrictions to simplify the implementation of the interface. And the result can be an interface that is easy to build but frustrating to use.

A series of design principles will be defined that allow the user to have control:

- Define interaction modes that do not force the user to perform unnecessary or unwanted actions.
- Consider flexible interaction.
- Allow user interaction to be interruptible and also reversible.
- Facilitate interaction as skill increases and allow interaction to be personalized.
- Hide internal technicalities from the casual user.
- Design direct interaction with objects that appear on the screen.

2. Reduce the need for the user to memorize

The more a user has to remember, the more error-prone their interaction with the system will be. A well-designed user interface will not tax the user's memory. Whenever possible, the system should "remember" the relevant information and help the user remember through an interaction scenario, the design principles that make it possible for an interface to reduce the user's memory load are defined:

- Reduce the demand for short-term memory.

When users are involved in complex tasks, demanding short-term memory can be significant. The interface should reduce requirements and remember previous actions and results.

- Make the preset meaningful.

The initial set of default values should be useful to the user, but users should also be able to specify their preferences.

- Define intuitive shortcuts. When the mnemonic is used to design a system (for example, alt-P to invoke the print function), it should be linked to an action that is easy to remember (for example, the first letter of the task) is invoked).
- The visual layout should be based upon a real-world metaphor. For example, in a bill payment system, the checkbook and check register metaphor should be used to guide the user through the bill payment process.
- Disclose information progressively.

The interface must be organized hierarchically. Information about a task, object, or behavior must first be presented at a high level of generalization. After the user indicates interest in the mouse, more details must be given. For example, you have the underline function for many word-processing applications. The function itself is one of several in the text-style menu. However, each of the underlining tools is not listed. The user must click the underline option; then, all the options for this function are presented (one line, double line, dotted line, etc.).

3. Make the interface consistent.

The interface must present and retrieve information consistently. This implies:

1) that all information is organized according to design rules that are respected on all displayed screens,
2) that input mechanism is limited to a small set used consistently throughout the application,
3) The mechanisms for moving from one task to another are defined and implemented consistently.
4) These rules of thumb form the basis for the user interface design principles guiding this very important software design activity.

Menu Schemes

Menus provide users with an easy and familiar way to retrieve information and interact with the system. Users are presented with the complete design of the system through a top-down diagram, where the different options that the system will have been shown.

A main feature of menus is typically to take the user through a series of submenus that provide various options.

In the menu scheme, it is important to make clear the different subsystems that the system will contain and each important option that corresponds to it, such as adding, modifying, deleting records, backups, updates, etc.

In addition, it is crucial to reflect on the type of information that can be consulted or the reports that can be generated.

Menus reduce the need for syntactic training and memorization and increase user task-relevant semantic knowledge.

The classification of menu schemes can be simple, serial, tree, network, and integrated.

Menus are an excellent way to allow users to select items from a list, but menus do not handle some tasks like data entry very well.

For this case, the best design method is filling out forms.

Screens Layout

Forms are used to get work done and enter data into the system.

When doing a forms analysis, you need to determine what data you are trying to capture, how it will be classified and entered into the form, who will capture the data and for what purpose, who will get a copy, and what should appear on the form. Copies, under what conditions the form will be filled out, how it will be handled, and how long it will be kept on file.

Paper forms remain the primary vehicles used to enter data into the system.

Several factors must be considered when selecting the paper to support the form: how long the form will be kept, the appearance of the form, the number of times it will be handled (e.g., an average of 6 times a day for a month), how it will be handled (e.g., worn by the user), its exposure to the environment (e.g., grease, dirt, heat, etc.), the fill-in-the-blank method used (manual, machine, etc.) and its security against deletion

Guidelines for form design:

1. Make the forms easy to fill out.
2. Please make sure the shapes meet the purpose for which they were designed.
3. Design shapes that ensure accurate filling.
4. The forms must be attractive.

Graphical Design Notation

Useful graphical tools include UML activity diagrams and flowcharts, useful graphical patterns that easily illustrate procedural details.

The activity diagram represents the sequence, condition, and repetition - all the elements that structured programming consists of - and is a descendant of an earlier graphic desh is still widely used) called a flowchart. In this diagram, similarly, a rectangle is used to indicate a step or processing. A diamond represents a logical condition, and arrows indicate control flow.

These are the same representations that are used in a flowchart.

Activities Diagram

The activity diagram represents the system from another perspective and thus complements the previous diagrams.

Graphically an activity diagram will be a set of arcs and nodes.

From a conceptual point of view, the activity diagram shows how control flows from one class to another to culminate in a total control flow corresponding to achieving a more complex process.

For this reason, actions and activities corresponding to different classes will appear in an activity diagram. Collaborating with all of them to achieve the same goal.

Example: Place an order.

An activity diagram contains the following:

- activity states
- transitions
- Decision
- sync bar
- streets
- Entity Flow

Activity State – Represents the execution of a procedure or the operation of activity in a workflow

Decision: they indicate which transition to follow after the completion of an activity, according to the value of the defined guard condition. The decision icon can also show where alternative paths join again.

Synchronization Bars - To show parallel subflows. It allows the expression of concurrent threads in a business to use c processes. That is, subflows that occur in parallel. It also represents where concurrent threads rejoin and the activity that part of it is not executed if all concurrent threads have not finished.

Lanes (swimlanes): each one represents a responsibility throughout the process, carried out by a part of the organization (workers-Workers)

Entity Flow: This shows how business entities are generated and used within the workflow.

Heuristics for the construction of the Activity Diagram

- Don't try to show design elements. Focus on customer needs and not move into the solution space.
- Do not substitute activity diagrams for use case descriptions.
- Limit the level of complexity of each diagram. If there are more than 3 possible paths, use additional diagrams to improve understanding.
- Use lanes for different roles.
- If possible, one diagram per use case.

Flowcharts

- They are the graphic representation of the sequence of process activities in the algorithms. It consists of symbols to represent the steps of an algorithm. Each symbol has a meaning that represents an action to be followed, corresponding to a step of the algorithm. Each symbol is connected by arrows, called flow lines, that indicate the order in which the steps must be executed.

- Since a Flowchart is the graphical representation of an algorithm, it must also have the following:

Input-process-output:

- To better understand flowcharts, you have to respect the construction rules. When performing a manual test, take a set of meaningful input data and start walking the Flowchart from top to bottom and left to right, depending on the form represented, to see how the Flowchart behaves and if the results obtained are correct and consistent.

Application exercise:

- Find the area of a circle for any radius. The Flowchart that represents this example is as follows:

Tabular design notation:

- In many software applications, a module is required to evaluate a complex combination of conditions and select appropriate actions based on them. Decision tables provide a notation that translates the actions and conditions (described in the processing narrative or use case) into tabular form.

Decision rules:

Each combination of condition input and its corresponding action input constitutes a relationship called a decision rule. There are as many rules as there are different condition/action input pairs. The number of decision rules must cover all possible cases without repetitions or omissions.

Forms of construction:

- The number of decision rules uses the formula 2 n, where n is actually the number of possible conditions.
- To an input condition, only one decision or output condition corresponds.
- Several input conditions can correspond to one output condition.
- For a decision table to be well constructed, one and only one of the situations must be true at any given time.
- Each decision rule (column) is an if-then structure (if the input condition is met, then perform such or such actions) of the Boolean type of conditions, and the laws of Boolean algebra can be applied to it.
- The list of conditions can be put in any order.
- The list of actions must be put in the order in which they have to be executed.
- Specify an appropriate name for the table, describing its purpose.

Example:

Consider the example of developing a decision table to represent the choice of a candidate to apply for the position of receptionist at Lycos SA de CV.

The criteria for selecting the candidate are the following:

- female sex
- Experience in similar jobs for more than two years
- Single

In this example, the conditions array specifies the selection criteria for the receptionist position. Applied Conditions contains two condition alternatives: Y for successful and N for unsuccessful. (If it meets or does not meet the condition).

Since there are three conditions, we have 2 3, which gives us 8 possible combinations. To complete the table, the two possible alternatives are divided in half; condition 1, female, will have 4Y and 4N. Then condition 2, experience, will have the first 4Y, 2Y, and 2N and the other 4, 2Y, and 2N. The third condition will have an alternative to each.

To find the resulting array of actions, we apply AND table. The application is accepted only when the three conditions are fulfilled.

They are useful in cases where complex conditions need to be represented. They are easier to document than flowcharts.

If the conditions are complex, they are rendered on one page, while the flowcharts could be spread over many pages reducing readability.

Program Design Notation

The program design language (PDL), or pseudocode, incorporates a programming language's logical structure and the free-form expressiveness of a natural language.

A basic LDP syntax should include constructs for: defining components, describing the interface, making data declarations, structuring blocks, doing a conditional, loop, and input/output constructs.

The pseudocode can be designed in English. When you design in English, you have a set of instructions more like a programming language.

Among the instructions used in the English pseudocode, we have the following:

- Begin…. End/Start…. Stop. These instructions are used to start and end.
- Accept, read, and input: These statements are used to get input from a user.
- Display, write, print: These are used to present a result or an output.
- If… else: They are used to make decisions

Design At The Component Level

The component-level design takes place after the architecture design is complete. At this stage, the general structure of the data and the software program has been established. The goal is to translate the design model into operational software.

Component-level data design focuses on representing data structures that are directly accessed through one or more software components.

Components are expandable entities. They are not compiled into an application program but installed directly on an execution platform. Other components can access the methods and attributes defined in their interfaces.

Example. A data collection component model.

The following steps represent a set of common tasks for component-level design when applied to an object-oriented system:

- Step 1. Identify all the design classes that correspond to the problem domain. Using the requirements and architectural model, each class of analysis and component of the architecture is elaborated.
- Step 2. Identify all the design classes that correspond to the infrastructure domain. These classes are not described in the requirements model and are often lost from the architectural model; however, they should be described at this point.
- Step3. Craft all layout classes that are not reusable components. Elaboration requires that all interfaces, attributes, and operations necessary to implement the class be described in detail. While performing this task, design heuristics must be considered.
- Step 4. Describe persistent data sources (databases and files) and identify the classes required to manage them.
- Step 5. Develop and craft behavior representations for a class or component. UML state diagrams were used as part of the requirements model to represent observable behavior from outside the system and the more localized behavior of the individual analysis classes.
- Step 6. Draw deployment diagrams to give more details of the implementation. Deployment diagrams are part of the architecture design and are represented in descriptor form. During component-level design, deployment diagrams can be produced representing the location of key component packages.
- Step 7. Redesign each design representation at the component level and always consider alternatives.

Deployment Or Distribution Diagram

A deployment diagram shows the configuration of nodes that participate in the execution and the components that reside on them.

It is a physical object at the run time representing a computational resource that usually has memory and processing capacity. Nodes can contain objects or instances of the component.

A node typically represents a processor or device on which components can be deployed.

Example. Deployment diagram or Distribution of a user connecting to the Internet, which is composed of the following:

- The user requests the keyboard and the monitor that he wants to connect to the Internet.
- A web browser is installed on the workstation, which is the one that receives the user's request.
- The web browser sends a connection request message using an HTTP or HTTPS protocol to the web server.
- The web server receives the message in the web interface of the application layer and sends the request to the database interface to be consulted. The Interface sends a message to the database server and the log file where that process would be stored.
- And finally, the user's request reaches the database created in the MySQL database manager and hosted on the database server. This link is either through the TCP/IP protocol, local connection, or socket.

Here we have two nodes, the client and the server, each containing components. The client component uses an interface from one of the server components. The relationship between the nodes is displayed. We could associate a stereotype to this relationship to indicate what type of connection we have between the client and the server and modify its cardinality to indicate that we support different clients. Since components can reside in more than one node, we can place the component independently, without it belonging to any node, and relate it to the nodes in which it is placed.

Chapter 4: Phases Of A System Design

According to the Kendall & Kendall methodology, the life cycle of a system consists of seven parts: the first being the identification of the problem, the second is the identification of information requirements, the third is the analysis of the needs of the system, the fourth is the recommended system design, the fifth system development and documentation, the sixth test and maintenance and the last implementation and evaluation. Each phase is explained separately, but they are never carried out as isolated steps; some activities may be carried out simultaneously, and some could be repeated.

Phase I:

- Identification of problems, opportunities, and objectives
- Direct observation of the environment
- Interview application to collect information.
- Synthesize the information collected to build objectives
- Estimate project scope
- Identify if there is a need, problem or opportunity argued
- Document results
- Study the risks of the project
- Submit a traffic report

In the first phase, the analyst is in charge of identifying the organization's problems, detailing them, examining them, and evaluating the opportunities and objectives.

The analyst must critically and accurately identify and evaluate existing organizational problems. Most of the problems are detected by someone else when the analyst is requested to specify them.

Opportunities are situations that the analyst considers likely to improve using computerized information systems, giving organizations greater security and efficiency and gaining a competitive advantage. The analyst must identify the objectives; that is, the analyst must find out what the company is trying to achieve; it will be possible to determine if some functions of the information systems applications can contribute to the business reaching its objectives by applying them to problems or opportunities. Specific. The users, analysts, and system administrators who coordinate the project are involved in the first phase. The activities of this phase are interviews with those in charge of coordinating users, synthesizing the knowledge obtained, estimating the project scope, and documenting the results. The result of this phase is a feasibility report that includes the definition of the problem and a summary of the objectives. Management must decide whether to go ahead or cancel the proposed project.

Phase II:

- Determination of information requirements
- Review of objectives
- Identify the domain
- Investigate the reason why the current system is implemented
- Collect information on the procedures and operations that are currently carried out.

Specifically, detail: Who are those involved, the activity, business rules and restrictions, development environment of the activities, opportune moments of development of each function, and how the current procedures are carried out.

- Prepare a detailed and organized list of all procedures.
- Separate functional and non-functional requirements
- Add to the report of the first phase this new information

In this phase, the analyst strives to understand the information users need to carry out their activities. Among the tools used to determine the information requirements of a business are interactive methods such as interviews, sampling, the investigation of printed data, and the application of questionnaires; non-user-interfering methods such as observing the behavior of decision makers, their office environments, and wide-ranging methods such as prototyping.

This phase is useful for the analyst to confirm his idea of the organization and its objectives.

Those involved in this phase are the analyst and the users, generally the workers and managers of the operations area.

The analyst needs to know the details of the functions of the current system:

The who (the people involved), the what (the business activity), the where (the environment where the activities take place), the when (the right time), and the how (the way current procedures are carried out) of the business under study.

At the end of this phase, the analyst must know how the business works and have complete information about the people, objectives, data, and procedures involved.

PHASE III:

- Needs analysis
- Evaluate the two previous phases.
- Model the inputs, processes, and outputs of the functions already identified.
- Elaborate data dictionary and its specifications.
- Develop process diagrams for each function.
- Prepare a system proposal with all the operations and process diagrams.
- Carry out the risk analysis on the one carried out in the previous phases, taking into account the economic, technical, and operational aspects (feasibility study)
- Estimate on a Gantt chart the time it will take to develop the system.
- In this phase, the analyst evaluates the previous two phases and uses tools and techniques such as data flow diagrams to graph the business functions' inputs, processes, and outputs in a structured graphical form.
- A data dictionary is developed from the data flow diagrams that list all the data used in the system and their respective specifications.
- In this phase, the analyst prepares the proposal of a system that synthesizes his findings, provides a cost/benefit analysis of the alternatives, and offers, where appropriate, recommendations on what to do.

PHASE IV:

- Design of the recommended system
- Evaluate the three previous phases.
- Perform the logical design of the entire system.
- Develop precise procedures for capturing the data that will enter the information system.
- Develop the database design.
- Design the different user interfaces for each operation, Procedure, and function.
- Design controls and backup procedures that protect the system and data.
- Produce specific software packages for programmers.
- Make a list of the generic functions and those that will be mandatory.

- Facilitates efficient data entry into the information system through appropriate form and screen design techniques. The analyst designs precise procedures for data capture that ensure that the data entered into the information system is correct.
- It also includes the design of files or databases that will store a large part of the data essential for those in charge of making decisions in the organization.
- In this phase, the analyst interacts with users to design the output (on-screen or printed) that meets the information needs of the latter.
- Finally, the analyst must design maintains and backup procedures that protect the system and data and produce program specification packages for programmers.
- Each package must contain schemas for input and output, file specifications, and processing details.

PHASE V:

- Software development and documentation
- Evaluate the procedures that the programmer will develop.
- Show and explain each Procedure, function, and operation to the programmer.
- Prepare manuals of internal procedures of the system.
- Prepare external help manuals for system users.
- Develop demonstrations for users and interact with different interfaces.
- Prepare updates for the different procedures
- Prepare a report with the time it took to build each Procedure.

In the fifth phase of the systems development cycle, the analyst works closely with the programmers to develop any necessary original software. Structured techniques for designing and documenting software include structure diagrams, Nassi-Shneiderman diagrams, and pseudocode.

During this phase, the analyst works with the users to create effective documentation for the software, such as how-to manuals, online help, and websites that include answers to frequently asked questions in "readme" files that will be integrated with the new software.

The documentation tells users how to use the system and what to do in case of problems arise from its use.

PHASE VI:

- Testing and maintenance of the system

- Schedule system tests.
- Make an instrument to evaluate the information system.
- The programmer should prepare a summary of the system tests.
- The analyst should make a report of his tests and discuss it with the programmer.
- Prepare the Planning of system maintenance hours.
- Prepare the list of operations that could undergo code modifications.

Before putting the system into operation, it is necessary to test it; it is much less expensive to find the problems before the system is delivered to the users.

Some of the testings is done by the programmers alone, and some are done jointly with systems analysts. First, the tests are carried out with sample data to determine the problems, and later, another is carried out with real data of the current system.

The information system's maintenance and documentation begin at this stage and are carried out routinely throughout its useful life.

PHASE VII:

- Implementation and evaluation of the system
- Gradually plan the conversion of the previous system.
- Install the necessary hardware equipment for the operation of the created software.
- Train users through workshops in the management of equipment and software created.
- Evaluate the adaptability of users to the system.

This is the last phase of systems development, and the analyst participates in implementing the information system. In this phase, users are trained in the management of the system. Some of the training is provided by the manufacturers, but supervision of this is the responsibility of the systems analyst.

Evaluation as the final phase of the mentioned systems development life cycle is mentioned primarily in discussion areas. In reality, evaluation takes place during each of the phases.

Systems work is cyclical; when an analyst finishes one phase of systems development and moves on to the next, the emergence of a problem could force them to return to the previous phase and modify the work done.

Chapter 5: How Can I Do A System Design Interview?

System design interviews typically last 45-60 minutes and begin with a very broad message, such as "Design Twitter." You will then be expected to generate a high-level design, showing the different system components that will be required, how they are connected, and any trade-offs in the approach you have taken.

Interview system design template:

1. Requirements. functional.
2. Storage estimate. Depending on the data modality: A rough estimate of the amount of data to be stored: to know what database can be used and file storage to store images/videos.
3. Database design.
4. High-level system design.
5. Additional components (optional)

How is the system design done?

A Step-by-Step Approach to Refining Your Interview System Design

1. Step 1: Understand the goals.
2. Step 2: Set the scope.
3. Step 3: Design for the correct scale.
4. Step 4: Start high, then go deeper.
5. Step 5: Data Structures and Algorithms (DS&A)
6. Step 6—Compensations.

What are the steps of system design?

The seven phases of the system design

- Planning.
- Systems and Requirements Analysis.
- System design.
- Development.
- Integration and Tests.
- Implementation.
- Operations and maintenance.

What are the components of the system design?

The following are the elements of a system design.

- Capabilities. Definition of the business and technology capabilities provided by the system.
- Processes. Design and redesign of business processes.
- Architecture.
- Data.
- Events.
- Business rules.
- Applications.
- Services and Components.

How do you practice systems design?

Three Reasons Should be Practiced System Design in Pramp

1. Practice asking the right questions to break down the requirements. It is critical to clear up ambiguities early on by asking the right questions.
2. Demonstrate your understanding of real-world tradeoffs.
3. Adapt to new requirements.

How is the system design done?

Definition: System design is the process of defining system elements such as modules, architecture, components, and consequently their interfaces and then data for a system based on specified requirements. A bottom-up or top-down approach must account for all related system variables.

What is a class design?

A design class describes a series of objects which share the same responsibilities, relationships, operations, attributes, and semantics.

What do you need to know about system design?

The study of the system is essential to design any system. The three most important aspects of system study are: identifying current problems and setting new goals. Study of an existing system. Document the existing system. 20) What is the step-by-step process for solving specific problems called?

Why do engineers struggle with system design interviews?

Engineers struggle with system design interviews (SDI) primarily for the following two reasons: Their lack of experience developing large-scale systems. Unstructured nature of IDEs.

How do we practice system design and object-oriented design?

Practice these common object-oriented design and systems design problems and interview questions.

Top 10 System Design Interview Questions

If you want to land on the job of your dreams at some big tech company (especially as a senior engineer), then your focus on building a large, complex, scalable system should count. There is no standard or precise answer to design interview questions.

You can have different conversations with different interviewers. Due to a lack of experience building a large-scale system and the open-ended nature of system design, many candidates struggle with this round.

1. Design a URL shortening service (TinyURL)
   - The service should generate a shorter, more unique alias given a long URL.
   - The service should redirect to the link when the user accesses a short link.
   - Consider scalability if thousands of URL-shortening requests arrive every second.
   - Service identifier redirects.
   - Support for custom short URLs.
   - Click statistics tracking.
   - Remove expired URLs.
   - The system must have high availability.

You should consider three things when designing this service.

   - API (REST API): Ask how the client will follow an approach for communicating with the service in conjunction with the load balancer, which is the service's front end.
   - Application Layer: Discuss how the worker thread or hosts will take the long URL, generate the small URL and store both URLs in the database.
   - Persistence Layer: Database
2. a global video streaming application

The service must be scalable so that many users can view and share the videos simultaneously. I'm going to store and transmit petabytes and petabytes of data.

Things to discuss and analyze:

- Approach to record video statistics, for example, the total number of views, votes for/against, etc.
- Add comments on videos in real-time.

Components:

- OC: Clouds like AWS and OpenConnect act as content delivery networks.
- Backend -Database
- Client: any device to use Youtube / Netflix

3. Design Facebook Messenger or WhatsApp
- Approach for one-on-one text messages between users.
- Approach to extend the design to support group chats.
- The state delivered and read
- What action to take if the user is not connected to the Internet?
- push notification
- Sending media such as images or other documents
- Approach to provide end-to-end message encryption.

4. Design Quora / Reddit / HackerNews

These services allow users to post questions, share links, and answer other users' questions. Users can also comment on shared questions or links.

Things to discuss and analyze:

- Approach to record statistics of each answer, such as the number of visits, votes for/against, etc.
- Follow options must be available for users to follow other users or topics.
- News generation means that users can see the list of top questions from all users and the topics that follow on their timelines.

5. Design Search Typehead

The type-ahead service allows users to type some query, and based on that, and it suggests the most searched items starting with whatever the user has typed.

Things to discuss and analyze:

- Approach to storing previous search queries
- Real-time system requirement
- Approach to keeping data up to date.
- Approach to find the best matches with the string already written
- Queries per second are to be handled by the system.
- Selection criteria for suggestions.

6. Design a web crawler

Design a scalable web crawler service that collects information (crawls) from across the web, fetching hundreds of millions of web documents.

Things to discuss and analyze:

- Focus on finding new web pages.
- Approach to prioritize dynamically changing web pages.
- Make sure the tracker is not unlimited on the same domain.

7. Design Facebook, Twitter, or Instagram

It is necessary to design a means of social communication and service for one billion users. Most interviewers spend time discussing the news generation service on these apps.

Features to consider:

- Some of the Twitter/Facebook/Instagram-specific features will be supported.
- Privacy controls around each tweet or post.
- The user must be able to post tweets, and the system must support replies to tweets/grouping tweets.

Components:

- News generation.
- Social graph (networking of friends between users or who follows who? - especially when millions of users follow a celebrity)
- Efficient storage and search of posts or tweets.

8. Design Uber

Design a service where a client requests a cab from the application, and a taxi driver arrives to take them to their desired destination. A frequent interview question in the systems design interview round.

Things to analyze and discuss:

- The backend mainly caters to mobile phone traffic. The uber app talks to the backend over mobile data.
- How does the dispatch system work (GPS / location data drives the dispatch system)? How to efficiently match user requests to nearby controllers?
- How do maps and routes work in Uber? How are ETAs calculated?
- An efficient approach to store millions of geographic locations for drivers/passengers who are always on the go.
- Approach to handle millions of updates to the driver location.
- Dispatch is primarily built with Node.js
- Services: Business logic services written primarily in Python.
- Databases: PostgreSQL, Redis, MySQL.

9. Design an API rate limiter (Github)

Design a service or tool that controls the number of requests per time window the service agrees to allow.

Things to analyze and discuss:

- Rate limiting will work for a distributed setup since the APIs are available across a group of servers.
- How to handle choke (soft and hard choke, etc.).

Tips For Going Through Systems Design

As you analyze your answers to the standard systems design interview questions above, try the following tips to get ready for your interview:

- Understand goals

Ask probing questions that help you understand who the users will be, what they need, and what the inputs and outputs of the system will be. Asking about these basics will help you stay focused and demonstrate your product sensibility and teamwork.

Use your experience to your advantage

You bring a unique set of values and knowledge that no one else has. Instead of trying to please what you think is needed, showcase your experience and show that you are valuable and irreplaceable due to your skills and abilities.

- Practice Matters

Using these tips to take design interviews repeatedly will help you build confidence, and familiarity with the topic will show your qualifications. Spend time rehearsing interview questions with a friend or in front of a mirror.

Discover the best Indeed resources for tech talent, including career tips, resume samples, quick links to job searches, and more.

Chapter 6: Guide to Cracking the System Design Interview

While looking for a job, I made a discovery. All developer articles about preparing for technical interviews seem to focus on coding. But the key to good money is successfully passing interviews where system design is discussed. You can either pass or fail coding interviews because you either find the solution you need or don't. But systems design interviews are different in this regard. They have more gradations and more answers.

It should also be said that interviews related to systems design allow you to separate junior developers from senior developers. Coding tasks are designed to test whether you can write code. And the system design tasks test your ability to write programs.

When interviewing for senior full-stack developer positions, I noticed that not all companies tested my knowledge of data structures and algorithms. Still, every interview had questions related to system design. All in all, these interviews are important.

And honestly, I think it's cool. In my practice, there were failures in such interviews, but there were also successfully passed interviews. In several interviews, it was felt how interesting it was to design a system.

In this chapter, I will tell you what questions I asked when interviewing developers in my old team. I will also show how juniors' answers differ from seniors' answers. And, of course, I will give recommendations on how to prepare for such interviews.

What interviews are you talking about?

First of all, let's break down what a system design interview is. This is an interview where the candidate is asked to design the software from start to finish. In its most basic form, the task can be formulated as "Design Twitter." And the candidate is given, say, an hour to imagine how he would design Twitter, including the data model and API. In some interviews, the candidate is directed: the interviewer draws the existing architecture on the whiteboard, and the candidate has to expand on the project. But often, the candidate has to start from scratch and design the entire product during the interview.

What is meant by "design from start to finish"? This is exactly what distinguishes juniors from seniors. Your perspective is not very broad when you are new to software development. Naturally, you focus on implementation details. Most of your time can be spent discussing the structure of classes in an application and the data model. The senior will touch on these issues, but he will also talk about such things as database replication schemes and load balancers. Scale difference.

- How to answer system design questions

Here is my algorithm for solving system design problems:

1. Clarify the issue and know the scope of the product.
2. Draw the most basic infrastructure.
3. Define API between server and client.
4. Define the database schema.
5. Optimize performance and availability.

The answer, of course, depends on the interview format, but if you have not been given a rigid structure, it is quite possible to use this sequence of steps. Let's see how this looks in practice.

Case Studies
Twitter

Let's extend this to a practical example of creating services like Twitter. Below are some questions regarding the Twitter design that should be answered before the next step:

- Our service user can post text and track other people.
- Should we design to create and display user timelines?on Twitter
- Will it contain photos and videos?
- Do we only pay attention to the back ends or the beginning of development? The user
- can search for text.
- Do we need to show hot trending topics?
- New (or important) transfer messages? All these questions will determine our final design.

Step 2: Evaluate the Back of the Envelope Estimating the scope of the system we will be designing has always been a good idea. It will also help to focus on later extensions, partitions, load balance, and cache. Expected system size

- (e.g., number of new messages, number of message views, number of timelines per second, etc.)? How much storage space do you need? We will have different retention requirements if the user's post contains photos and videos.
- Are we supposed to use web width? This is necessary to decide how to manage the flow and load balance between the servers.

Phase 3: System Interface Definition

Determines which APIs are required for the system. This will establish the exact contract the system expects to enter and ensure we have not received any erroneous requirements. Below is an example of our Twitter service:

postTweet(user_id, tweet_data, tweet_location, user_location, timestamp, ...)

generateTimeline(user_id, current_time, user_location, ...)

markTweetFavorite(user_id, tweet_id, timestamp, ...)

Step 4: Model to define the data. The data

The model that defines the data at the start of the interview will refine how data moves between the various components of the system. Later it will guide the data section and management. Candidates must define various system structures, how they will interact, and various aspects of data management, such as storage, transmission, encryption, etc.

User: User ID, Name, Email, Dob, CreationDate, LastLogin, etc.

Twitter: Twitter ID, content, Twitter location, NumberOfLikes, Time Title.

UserFollow: UserID1, UserID2

FavoritetTweets: User ID, TweetID, Time Title

What database system should we use? Are HOOS like Cassandra the best fit for our needs, or should solutions like MySQL be used? What blocks should we use to store photos and videos?

Stage 5: High-level design Based on 5 - 6 blocks, a diagram was developed representing the main components of our system. We must define enough components to solve practical problems from end to end.

For Twitter, at a higher level, we need multiple application servers to serve all read/write requests preceded by a boot equalizer to distribute the stream. Assuming we have more of a read stream (compared to a write stream), we might decide to use a separate server to handle these scenarios. At the back end, we need an efficient database that stores all the messages and supports a large amount of reading. We also need a distributed file system to store photos and videos.

Stage 6: Detailed design

Deepen the excavation of two to three main components; feedback from inspectors should always guide us in understanding which parts of the system require further discussion. We must present the different approaches, their strengths, and weaknesses, and then argue why we prefer one approach instead of the other. Remember that there is no single answer; it is important to consider the balance between the various options while not forgetting the systemic limitations.

- Since we will store a large amount of data, how can we split it into multiple databases? Should one try to store all user data in one database? What is the problem?
- How will we handle frequently sent messages or pay attention to many popular users?
- Since the user's timeline will contain the latest (and related) text messages, should we try to save the data by optimizing the scanning of the latest messages?
- On which floor should we enter the cache to speed up the speed? What components need to be load balanced?

Step 7: Identify and Eliminate Bottlenecks Try to discuss as many bottlenecks as possible and various ways to eliminate them.

- Do we have a single-point fault in the system? what are we doing to alleviate this?
- Do we have enough copies of the data so that if some servers are lost, we can still serve the users?
- Similarly, do we have enough copies of various services so that some failures do not bring the system to a complete halt?
- How will we control the operation of the service? When key components fail or properties go down, do we get warnings?

Design a Facebook messenger

Why did I choose this question? Similar tasks were on interviews with my old team at Salesforce. Our product was also a messenger, although far from being so famous. Naturally, we expected seniors to have basic knowledge of how to chat applications work. If the candidate were unfamiliar with Facebook messenger, we would review the functionality of this application and tell the candidate what function he should design.

1. Clarify the issue and know the scope of the product

Your first question should be, "Which features should I focus on?". Then it would help if you asked how many users should be expected. The answers to these key questions will determine your project. The design of the database and API depends on the functionality, and the scale determines the best way to optimize.

For our purposes, let's say we're targeting 1 million messages per second, and from functionality, we should be able to send and receive messages and view the message history. The user can correspond with other users, and the correspondence history must be stored indefinitely.

2. Draw the most basic infrastructure

Any solution requires a server, a client, and a database. In this case, we will have two clients using the server as an intermediary for correspondence and a database for storing user information and message history.

All this is the basis of your scheme. Drawing such a small diagram may seem like a trivial task, but interviewers will understand you much better if you show the flow of data in the diagram when explaining the solution.

One important decision to make at this stage is what type of database you will be using. SQL or NoSQL? Be prepared to discuss the pros and cons of every option and justify your choice. Of course, you can use a NoSQL database, but we still use SQL because we want to bind messages to account IDs.

3. Define API between server and client

We have already said that we will focus on sending and receiving messages. What will the data movement look like for these purposes?

User A sends a message to the server. The server forwards the message to user B. User B receives the message displayed in his client.

We can take this verbal description and convert it to pseudocode.

//clients pseudocode

function sendMessage(message) {

```
  //REST call to post a message to our backend server

}


function receive message(message) {

  //we can receive the message via long poll, web socket, or server-side event

  //once the message is received, render it to the screen

}
//servers pseudocode


public void pass message(message, userA, userB) {

  //receive the message from User A via a REST post

  //store the message in the database

  //post the message to User B

}
```

Your interviewer may suggest specific scenarios for you to implement. For example, when conducting interviews like this, I often asked the candidate what he would do if the message did not go through. In such a case, you can modify the existing API methods to include exponential retry or add message resubmission as a feature with your API methods.

Having dealt with one function (messaging), you can move on to the next (viewing chat history).

4. Define the database schema

I want to emphasize that everything should be kept as simple as possible throughout the design process. At each step, try to reduce everything to the minimum viable product. The database schema is no exception to this rule.

Here's what a simple database schema for a messenger might look like:

There is a User entity containing the user ID and username and a Message entity containing the message ID, sender user ID, recipient user ID, message timestamp, and message body.

If the interviewer is interested, he will ask a clarifying question. Then you will tell what type of data will be in each column. But if you don't get asked about it, don't be the first to bring it up: that way, you avoid having to make a whole bunch of technical decisions.

5. Optimize performance and availability

So, you have a system that allows you to send and receive messages and store them. The next step is to identify bottlenecks.

Our system sends and receives messages between users and stores and retrieves messages from the database. Let's consider what can slow down each operation and how to fix it.

- Sending and receiving messages

How will we process a million messages per second? As a rule, one server can handle 50 thousand connections simultaneously. This means that we need 20 servers to process a million messages. To distribute requests equally, we'll add a load balancer that uses the round-robin algorithm to determine which client is directed to which server.

- Storing and retrieving messages

Since we are writing each message to the database, we will do a million writes per second. What about reading operations? We will need to retrieve messages from the database every time the user loads the page. But we cannot download the entire message history at once since the performance of such a request will be very low. We need to implement lazy loading to retrieve only a predetermined set of posts and then prompt for more posts as the user scrolls through history.

With that in mind, let's say we have 10,000 messages read every second, both when the user loads the page and when they scroll. This gives us a read/write ratio of 1/100, i.e., our system is dominated by write operations (write-heavy system). So we need to optimize the number of concurrent writes.

It is possible to split the database based on the hash of the sender ID and place the shards on different servers. This will reduce the contention of database connections since traffic will be evenly distributed between the shards. This will also contribute to the efficiency of message retrieval since two shards will need to be accessed to extract the history of each dialogue.

- Next steps

From my experience, I can judge that the steps described above will take up to 60 minutes of the interview. You can optimize availability by replicating the database or adding additional functionality if you have time. For example, you can implement a list of friends in the system.

Designing a search robot

This topic will focus on an interesting classic challenge encountered in IT system design interviews—creating a crawler.

A search robot is also called a web spider or web crawler. Search engines widely use it to discover new or updated content on the web. These can be web pages, images, videos, PDFs, etc. First, the crawler collects several web pages and then follows all the links they contain to collect new content.

The search robot is used for many different tasks.

- Indexing in a search engine. This is the most common use case. The robot collects web pages to create a local index for the search engine. For example, in the Google search engine, this role is played by Googlebot.
- Web archiving. It collects information from web pages for later storage and use. For example, many national libraries are archiving websites. Notable examples include the US Library of Congress and the EU Web Archive.
- Extracting web data. The super-rapid development of the Internet creates an unprecedented opportunity for information gathering. Web data mining helps you collect valuable information on the web. For example, leading financial firms use web crawlers to download transcripts of shareholder meetings and annual reports to analyze key company initiatives.
- Web monitoring. Web crawlers help track copyright infringement and trademark infringement on the Internet. For example, Digimarc looks for pirated copies and reports.

The complexity of developing a search robot depends on what scale it must support. Whether it's a modest school project that can be completed in a couple of hours or a gigantic system that requires constant attention from an entire team of engineers. Therefore, you first need to decide on the scope and features that should be supported.

Step 1: Understand the problem and define the scope of the solution

The search robot works according to a simple principle:

- The input is a list of URLs, after which the corresponding web pages are loaded.

- URLs are extracted from web pages.
- New URLs are added to the list for further download. These three steps are repeated anew.

Is the work of the search robot limited to this simple algorithm? Not really.

Designing a large-scale search robot is very difficult. It is unlikely that someone will be able to do this during an interview. Before moving on to the architecture, asking questions about the system's requirements and scale is necessary.

Candidate: "What is the main purpose of a search robot? Is it used for search engine indexing, data collection, or something else?

Interviewer: "For indexing in a search engine."

Candidate: "How many web pages do a crawler collect monthly?"

Interviewer: "1 billion pages."

Candidate: "What kind of content are we looking for? Only HTML or other resources like PDFs and images?

Interviewer: "Only HTML."

Candidate: "Should recently added or edited web pages be considered?"

Interviewer: "Yes."

Candidate: "Should the assembled HTML pages be stored?"

Interviewer: Yes. Shelf life is 5 years.

Candidate: "What to do with web pages with duplicate content?"

Interviewer: "They should be ignored."

These are just some of the questions you can ask an interviewer. It is necessary to understand the requirements and clarify incomprehensible points. Even if you are asked to design a product as simple as a crawler, you and the interviewer may have a different understanding of what it should be.

In addition to the functionality that needs to be agreed upon with the interviewer, the following characteristics of the search robot must be considered.

- Scalability. The internet is huge. It has billions of web pages. The crawler must be extremely efficient and use parallel computing.

- Sustainability. The Internet is full of traps. You will constantly encounter invalid HTML, unresponsive servers, crashes, malicious links, etc. The crawler must deal with all of these edge cases.
- Politeness. A crawler should not send too many requests to a website in a short amount of time.
- Expandability. The system must be flexible so that large changes do not have to be made to support new types of content. For example, if we need to collect graphic files in the future, this should not lead to reworking the entire system.

Rough estimates:

The following estimates are based on many assumptions, so you should ensure you and the interviewer understand each other correctly.

Let's say that 1 billion web pages are downloaded every month.

QPS: 1,000,000,000 / 30 days / 24 hours / 3600 seconds = ~400 pages per second.

Peak QPS = 2 * QPS = 800.

Let's assume that the average size of a web page is 500 KB.

1 billion pages * 500 KB = 500 TB per month of storage. If you're unfamiliar with data units, reread the Power of Two sections in Chapter 2.

If data is stored for five years, 500 TB * 12 months * 5 years = 30 Pb.For content collected over five years, you need 30 Pb of storage.

Step 2: offer a common solution and get an agreement

Having defined the requirements, we move on to general architectural issues.

Source URLs

The search process uses source URLs as a starting point. For example, we would start with the university's domain name to iterate over all the web pages on a university website.

To traverse the entire internet, we must choose source URLs creatively. A good source URL will allow you to iterate over as many links as possible. The general strategy is to divide the address space into separate parts. The first proposed approach is based on location, as the popularity of certain websites may vary by country. Source URLs can also be selected by topic. For example, the address space can be divided into shopping, sports, medical, and so on. The choice of source URLs depends on various factors.

Scan border:

Most modern search robots divide content into already downloaded and pending downloads. The component that stores the URLs to download is called a crawl boundary. It can be thought of as a first-in, first-out queue. In-depth information about this component can be found in the section on in-depth engineering.

HTML Loader

This component loads web pages from the Internet. The crawl boundary provides the URLs of these web pages.

DNS resolver

The URL must first be translated into an IP address to load a web page. To do this, the HTML loader can consult a DNS resolver. For example, as of March 5, 2019, the URL www.wikipedia.org is converted to the IP address 198.35.26.96.

Content Analyzer

After loading a web page, it needs to be analyzed: what if it has an incorrect HTML code that will cause problems and only take up storage space? Placing the content analyzer on the same server as the crawler will slow down the data collection. In this regard, it has the appearance of a separate component.

Existing content?

As an online study shows, 29% of all web pages are duplicates, which can lead to re-saving the same content. We use the "Existing content?" data structure to avoid duplication of information and reduce processing times. It helps to discover new content that the system has already stored. But this is a slow and time-consuming approach, especially regarding billions of web pages. To effectively perform this task, it is necessary to compare not the web pages themselves but their hashes.

Content storage

This is the HTML storage system. Its choice depends on data type and size, access frequency, lifetime, etc. Both disk and memory are used.

Most of the content is stored on disk because the data set is too large to fit in memory.

The requested content is stored in memory to reduce latency.

Link Extractor

This component parses HTML pages and extracts links from them.

URL Filter The URL

Filter rejects certain content types, file extensions, links to error pages, and blocklisted URLs.

Existing URL?

"Existing URL?" is a data structure that keeps track of URLs that have already been visited or are in the crawl boundary. This helps avoid re-opening the same URL, fraught with increased server load and potential endless loops.

Techniques such as the Bloom filter and hash table are commonly used to implement this component.

URL storage

This is a repository of already visited URLs.

So, we have considered each component. Now we will put them together and discuss the principle of the system as a whole.

1. Step 1: Add source URLs to the crawl boundary.
2. Step 2: The HTML loader takes the list of URLs from the crawl boundary.
3. Step 3: The HTML loader gets the appropriate IP addresses from the DNS resolver and starts loading.
4. Step 4. The content analyzer parses the HTML pages and checks their correctness.
5. Step 5: Once parsed and validated, the content is passed to the Existing Content. Component.
6. Step 6. Component "Existing content?" checks if the given HTML page is in the store:

- If there is, it means that this content is located at a different URL, and we have already processed it. in this case, the HTML page is rejected;

- if not, the system hasn't processed the content yet, so it's passed to the link extractor.
7. Step 7. Links are extracted from HTML pages.
8. Step 8: The extracted links are passed to the URL filter.
9. Step 9. After filtering, the links are passed to the "Existing URL?" component.
10. Step 10. Component "Existing URL?" checks if the URL is in the store. If yes, it has already been processed, and nothing else needs to be done.
11. Step 11: If the URL has not been processed, it is added to the crawl boundary.

Snapchat system design

Unlike Facebook and Twitter, which record and post everything you do, Snapchat uses messages that are supposed to disappear (see how they don't).

Important Design Terms

Monolithic architecture – A single-tier application that works independently of other applications is known as a monolith (monolithic architecture). A monolith is designed to perform and manage all the activities required to complete a task. The app performs all the functions from start to finish.

Microservices – It is the polar opposite of monoliths. Microservices is an architectural approach that organizes an application as basically a collection of services. These services are used to control many aspects of an application. A customer places an order, a waiter takes it and delivers it, and a chef prepares it. In this example, each component works independently and separately; nobody knows exactly what the others are doing, and nobody has access to the same information.

JSON – is a text-based format that can display JavaScript objects, literals, arrays, and data. This text-based format is intended to be easy to read and write and digestible by software. JSON is commonly used to transfer data and information between servers and online applications.

Orchestration: The technique of automating many operations is known as orchestration. These jobs include configuring, coordinating, and managing computer systems and software.

Proxy: It acts as an intermediary between a client seeking a resource and the server providing it.

Mesh: A service mesh is a software architecture pattern that adds a layer to an infrastructure layer to enable regulated, observable, and secure communication between services through a proxy.

Integration Of Additional Features

Snapchat's camera app has lenses, filters, emojis, and the ability to add augmented reality animations, among other things. The Snapchat chat app also allows users to store photos, save conversations, add emoticons, and more.

The Snapchat map, among other things, allows you to monitor your friends if they wish. Memories, photo editing, and content consumption are separate Snapchat apps with unique capabilities.

Memories allow you to store or modify photos or videos for later use and upload or send them. Users can also use image editing to cut movies, add text, add stickers, and more.

Snapchat's external content consumption refers to what it shows users based on various parameters.

Microservices

The program relied heavily on JSON for network queries at the time. However, parsing JSON was time-consuming and inefficient. Snapchat used a centralized network management API to mask the use of JSON as an implementation detail to address this issue.

Microservices present the challenges of application state management, service communication, and fault management. Snapchat used open-source technologies like Temporal to overcome orchestration difficulties to build a robust and reliable system.

As a result, the organization decided to use a service mesh design pattern. Snapchat used Envoy, another open-source proxy tool, to achieve this pattern. Envoy managed service traffic flow through the infrastructure, giving developers visibility into potential issues.

Snapchat created an internal app called Switchboard within the service network. The Switchboard served as a control panel for Snap's services, allowing users to switch traffic, manage service dependencies (a feature that allows one service to be managed depending on the condition of others), and drain regions.

To simplify the complexity of possible configurations within services, Switchboard was used instead of exposing the entire Envoy API. Thanks to the service network, Snap has a common internal and regional network for its microservices.

Services within the same region could connect without using the public Internet, and no external network traffic could communicate with internal network parts.

Only the Gateways would be authorized to be exposed to the Internet for security reasons. API gateways, for example, could easily serve as gateways, processing client/user requests and routing them along with the network.

Network Gateway And API

All queries from the Snapchat client come through the API Gateway. It uses the same Envoy image and connects to the same control plane as our internal microservices. Our Control Plane allows us to enable custom Envoy filters.

These filters control Snapchat's authentication systems and our speed-limiting and load-shedding technologies. Envoy uses Service Mesh to route requests to the relevant microservice once the filter chain is complete.

Stock Trading Platform

Using stock trading techniques, you can learn to trade stocks to make a living faster.

Additionally, stock trading systems can let you live the life you want by allowing you to trade stocks profitably with little work and stress.

A trading system is a collection of guidelines that specify how to enter and exit financial markets to generate income.

Building A Stock Trading Platform

A stock trading platform is significantly more difficult to build and needs specialized equipment for each task. In this post,

I have done my best to describe how a stock trading platform works.

Let us begin.

Requirements

- A share's purchase/sale price must be open to offers from users.
- The ability for users to see the ticker, or the real-time and historical price of the stock, is essential.
- Inform subscribers of changes in the price of shares.
- The system must be able to handle 100k clients.
- 100 million offers every day should be manageable for the system.
- The system must be able to provide historical stock price information.

Required Capacity

Stock exchanges are usually busy from 9 am to 5 pm. Thus, during the entire 8-hour window, traffic will be served.

Therefore, we can determine the capacity of the tender service for this period.

We can assume that the read-to-write ratio on the offers is 1:1.

High-Level Design

Taking bids from consumers is the responsibility of the bidding service.

The Ticker Service is responsible for displaying the most recent changes in the share price.

Offer Service

The bidding service must accept the user's bids to buy/sell and be able to locate buyers/sellers and execute the transaction.

When a buy/sell offer comes in, we need a matching engine that can match one or more buyers/sellers and then execute the transaction.

If the matching engine cannot do so, we need to store the offer and try again when the matching offer arrives.

The Quote Service

The ticker service must provide clients with the most recent stock price and be able to display historical data based on the passage of time.

It is necessary to determine the current stock price from the completed transactions of the bidding service and maintain it in the historical price database.

For the ticker service to calculate the most recent stock price, we need transactions that occurred in the Stock DB.

We can use a design pattern called Change Data Capture in this situation.

Data Center

In my experience, people frequently choose the DB first and try to force-fit their case.

We should always determine the needs of each database in our services and then select the data store accordingly, ideally based on query pattern, scalability, and reliability, among other factors.

Auction Shop

It should have the capacity to host billions of offers.

Data must be able to be stored and retrieved with minimal latency and high QPS.

The criteria mentioned above should be met with an in-memory fragmented data store.

Stock Trading Warehouse

Ideally, the transaction should be stored with the ACID guarantee.

If a bid to buy matches multiple bids to sell, you should be able to allow multiple deals to be committed.

We can select any Datastore with an ACID guarantee for this use case.

Old Price Shop

The price of a share should be able to be stored based on the current time.

We can select any store that offers recovery based on time series.

Data Division

Proper partitioning of data is a crucial component of scalability. So that data growth is not a problem.

It would be best if you now had a basic understanding of how to build a stock trading platform. Now let's talk about the platform's key components that need to be considered.

Key Components

- Selecting A Programming Language

Now, depending on the platform for your application, you have to choose a programming language.

Therefore, various programming languages are available, although some are more popular than others.

Developers prefer Swift or Objective C for iOS, while Kotlin and Java are the most popular choices among professionals for Android.

Front End Technologies

Business application developers choose their technology stack after having a clear idea of the finished product.

The front, back-end, and DevOps sides of a typical web-based platform make up the platform. React.js plus Angular are currently the most used technologies for front-end development.

Both work well for stock market software development and are appropriate for large-scale projects.

Certain technical details can influence developers to go a certain way. For example, Angular draws attention with its wide range of services.

Because it is an established framework, angular provides all the necessary elements for front-end development. In contrast, React is a library. It would help if you used third-party tools to implement certain functionality.

Back-End Technologies

My preference for the back end is between Java and . NET. Enterprise-grade application development and trading platforms are a perfect fit for both technologies.

They support numerous procedures in the program and help in the implementation of sophisticated logic.

Java and .NET are also very similar in terms of performance and speed. Because of this, choosing one option or another depends entirely on the nature of a given project.

Application Programming Interface

The software that supports the operation of your trading platform is connected through the API.

Therefore, the application can implement your best business plans thanks to a robust API system. Several steps to understand:

•   Use technologies like Swagger, Kong, Postman, etc., that allow faster processing and better management of APIs.

•   For seamless scalability of the application and to host an API, AWS or Firebase are used.

•   API security is also essential, and key risk mitigation strategies should include encryption, gateways, and throttling.

•   Using the most appropriate and efficient RDBMS and API database management software.

•   Use API programming to build apps for all platforms, whether Android, iOS, or web-based.

System Design For Transmission Services

System Requirements

Among the most popular video streaming services in the world are YouTube and Netflix. To improve the user experience, its architecture includes a series of elements.

Such a service includes popular movies, billing, AI-based recommendation systems, and watch-later features, but we'll focus on the essentials.

Fundamental Qualities

We have included the following capabilities in our concept for a streaming video service:

- Content creators can post videos.
- Viewers can use many devices to watch videos (mobile, TV, etc.).
- On videos, users can comment, like, or dislike.
- Video titles can be used to search for videos.
- The system may store views, likes, and dislikes to display these statistics to users.

System Goals

- There should be no buffering so viewers can watch videos in real-time.
- Video storage must be reliable. You should not lose the videos you have uploaded.
- With an increase in users, the system should be scalable.
- Low latency and high availability should be features of the system. Consistency isn't that important in this situation because it's okay for a user to wait a while before watching a newly submitted movie.

A single server cannot handle the volume of data as the system must handle heavy traffic regularly. A group of servers will be used to service the system.

There should be no noticeable speed hit to clients, even if a server fails.

High-Level Architecture

A streaming video program can accept one of three different types of requests:

- upload (write)
- Search (read)
- see (read)

Since read queries (search and view) are often more frequent than write requests (load), each is handled by a separate server group.

Because the program is read intensive, you will need to configure more servers to handle read requests than loads.

Each request made by a client is routed to the appropriate microservice by the load balancer when it is received.

Upload Service

The upload service, which processes the video, uploads it to the Open Connect servers, and makes it accessible to all users, fulfills an upload request.

Search Service

The load balancer sends the search request to the search microservice, which then sends it to Netflix Elastic Search. The client receives the search response from Elastic.

Netflix uses Elastic Search, an incredibly scalable full-text open-source search engine, to search millions of videos.

Netflix uses elastic search to analyze customer service operations.

See Service

Most viewing requests will not be sent to the load balancer or Netflix servers. Instead, users will connect to local ISPs and be fed directly from the nearest Open Connect server.

However, if the requested video cannot be accessed, it will be sent to the load balancer and view microservice.

The video is then fetched from the metadata database, retrieved from the path specified in the metadata, and streamed to the client.

Of course, this technique includes latency, so virtually all display requests are served over Open Connect.

Upload Videos

The main purpose of YouTube is to upload a movie or a video. A video streaming service must overcome some hurdles before a video is accessible to its consumers.

Keep In Pieces

Each video sent will be split into numerous smaller files instead of being kept as one huge file.

This is essential as content producers can submit huge videos. A single large file can take a while to process or transmit.

The viewer will not have to download the entire video to play it if it is saved and made available in parts.

To ensure that there is low latency between chunks and that the user has a smooth viewing experience, the client will first request the first chunk from the server and then request the next chunk while that chunk is playing.

Processing Queue

Each video has numerous chunks, and Netflix will use multiple concurrent workers to parse them, so a render queue is required. Adding them to the queue is simplified.

Jobs will be collected by workers (or coders, which we'll cover next), encoded into various formats, and then stored in distributed file storage.

Video Encoding

It is crucial to convert and save the video clips in various formats so that viewers can access them using the technology and internet connection that works best for them.

Viewers can watch the video on a laptop, phone, TV, or other devices. The optimal formats for various devices differ from each other.

Similarly, multiple viewers could use multiple bandwidths to access the Internet.

Some viewers can stream high-resolution movies easily, depending on their internet connection speed or bandwidth. In contrast, those with lower bandwidth will be able to stream low-quality videos much more easily.

Open Connect

When you use your browser to request Netflix.com, you ask your ISP (Internet Service Provider) to start a connection between your computer and the Netflix server.

Your ISP contacts Netflix's IP address on your behalf and returns the result to you. The audience in a remote nation like Tokyo will experience significant delays in transmitting and receiving signals due to the concentration of these servers in the US.

With videos, delays are much more of a concern, as a lot of data has to be transmitted to the viewer, and if so, the transmission will be delayed, and the user experience will suffer.

Netflix uses a clever technique to fix the problem. It is known as Open Connect (OC). Open Connect is the CDN used by Netflix (Content Delivery Network).

Load Balancing

A single application server cannot handle the volume of requests (including load, search, and display requests) that arrive every second.

There must be a load balancer to effectively distribute the workload across the many servers, as multiple servers are involved.

Netflix employs constant hashing to distribute loads across servers because it can handle server failures and accommodate the installation of additional servers with ease.

Since the popularity of each video varies, the actual servers hosting these movies could experience uneven load. By using dynamic HTTP redirects, which allow a busy server to redirect a new request to an open server, we can solve this problem.

Autonomous Vehicle System Design

High-Level System Architecture

The essential sensors, actuators, hardware, and software are listed in the architecture, demonstrating AVs' entire communication mechanism or protocol.

Perception

This stage comprises identifying the location of the AV relative to the environment and sensing the environment around the AV using a variety of sensors.

The AV uses RADAR, LIDAR, a camera, real-time kinetics (RTK), and other sensors in this step. The reconnaissance modules receive the data from these sensors and process it after transmission.

The AV generally consists of a control system, LDWS, TSR, unknown obstacle recognition (UOR), a vehicle positioning and localization (VPL) module, etc.

The combined information is delivered to the decision-making and planning stage after processing.

Decision And Planning

The movements and behavior of the VA are decided, planned, and controlled in this step using the information received during the perception process.

This stage represents the brain, where decisions are made about route planning, action prediction, obstacle avoidance, etc.

The choice is based on information that is now and historically accessible, including real-time map data, traffic details, trends, user information, etc.

A data logging module could keep track of errors and data for later use.

Sterilization

The control module executes operations/actions related to the physical control of the AV, such as steering, braking, acceleration, etc., after receiving information from the decision and planning module.

Chassis

The last step is to interact with the mechanical parts fixed to the chassis, such as the Gearmotor, the steering wheel motor, the brake pedal motor, and the accelerator and brake pedal motors.

The control module signals and manages all these components.

We will now discuss general AV communication before discussing several key sensors' design, operation, and use.

RADAR

RADAR scans the environment in AVs to find and locate cars and other objects.

RADARs are often used for military and civil purposes, such as airports or weather systems, and operate in the millimeter-wave (mm-Wave) spectrum.

Different frequency bands, including 24, 60, 77, and 79 GHz, are used in contemporary automobiles and have a measurement range of 5 to 200 m [10].

The distance between the VA and the object is determined by calculating the ToF between the transmitted signal and the returned echo.

In AVs, RADARs employ an array of micro antennas that create a collection of lobes to improve range resolution and multiple target identification. Millimeter wave RADAR can accurately assess short-range objects in any direction using the variation in Doppler shift due to its higher penetrability and higher bandwidth.

Since mm-Wave radars have a longer wavelength, they have anti-jamming and anti-pollution capabilities that allow them to work in the rain, snow, fog, and low light.

Also, the Doppler shift can be used to calculate relative velocity via millimeter-wave radars. Due to their capability, millimeter wave radars are suitable for various AV applications, including obstacle detection and pedestrian and vehicle recognition.

Ultrasonic Sensors

These sensors work in the range of 20 to 40 kHz and use ultrasonic waves. A magnetoresistive membrane that can measure the distance of the object produces these waves.

The distance is determined by calculating the time of flight (ToF) of the emitted wave to the echo signal. The typical range of ultrasonic sensors is less than 3 meters.

The sensor output is updated every 20 ms, which prevents it from meeting the stringent quality of service requirements of ITS. These sensors have a relatively small beam detection range and are aimed.

Therefore, to obtain a full field view, numerous sensors are required. However, many sensors will interact and can result in significant range inaccuracies.

LiDAR

The 905 and 1550 nm spectra are used in LiDAR. Since the human eye is susceptible to retinal damage in the 905nm range, current LiDAR operates in the 1550nm band to reduce retinal damage.

Up to 200 meters is the maximum working range of LiDAR. Solid state, 2D, and 3D LiDAR are the different subcategories of LiDAR.

A single laser beam scatters off a rapidly rotating mirror in a 2D LiDAR. A 3D LiDAR can acquire a 3D image of the surroundings by placing multiple lasers in the capsule.

A roadside LiDAR system has been proved to reduce the number of vehicle-to-pedestrian (V2P) collisions in both intersectional and non-intersectional areas.

It employs a computationally effective, real-time, 16-line LiDAR system.

It is suggested to use an artificial neural network deep autoencoder (DA-ANN) encoder, which achieves an accuracy of 95% at 30 m.

It is demonstrated how an algorithm which is based on a support vector machine (SVM) combined with a 3-line 64D LiDAR can improve pedestrian recognition.

Despite having better measurement accuracy and 3D vision than millimeter wave radar, LiDAR performs less well in harsh weather conditions such as fog, snow, and rain.

Cameras

Depending on the wavelength of the device, the camera in AVs can be based on visible or infrared light.

Depending on the lens's quality, the camera's maximum range is around 250m. The three bands used by visible cameras (red, green, and blue) are separated by the same wavelength as the human eye, or 400 to 780nm (RGB).

Two VIS cameras with set focal lengths are coupled to create a new channel containing depth information (D), allowing the creation of stereoscopic vision.

A 3D view of the area around the vehicle can be obtained through this capability through the camera (RGB-D).

The infrared (IR) camera uses passive sensors ranging between 780nm and 1mm. In maximum illumination, IR sensors in AV offer visual control.

This camera helps AVs with object recognition, side view control, accident recording, and BSD. However, the camera's performance is affected in adverse weather conditions, such as snow, fog, and changing light conditions.

The main benefits of a camera are its ability to accurately collect and record the texture, color distribution, and shape of the environment.

Global Navigation Satellite System And Global Positioning System, Inertial Measurement Unit

This technology helps the AV navigate by pinpointing its precise location. GNSS uses a group of satellites in orbit around the planet's surface to locate.

The system stores data about the AV's location, speed, and precise time.

It works by calculating the ToF between the received signal and the satellite emission. Global Positioning System (GPS) coordinates are often used to obtain AV locations.

GPS-derived coordinates are not always accurate and typically add a positional error with a mean value of 3m and a standard variance of 1m.

In metropolitan situations, performance deteriorates further, with location error of up to 20m, and in certain severe circumstances, GPS position error is approximately 100m.

In addition, AVs can use the RTK system to determine the vehicle's position accurately.

In autonomous vehicles, the position and direction of the vehicle can also be determined by dead reckoning (DR) and inertial position.

Sensor Fusion

For proper vehicle management and security, AVs must gain accurate, real-time knowledge of vehicle location, health, and other factors such as weight, stability, speed, etc.

This information must be collected by AVs using a variety of sensors.

The fusion technique produces consistent information by fusing the data acquired from multiple sensors.

The method allows the synthesis of raw data acquired from complementary sources.

As a result, sensor fusion enables the AV to accurately understand its surroundings by merging all the useful data collected from various sensors.

Different algorithms, including Kalman and Bayesian filters, are used to carry out the fusion process in VAs.

Because it is used in various applications, including RADAR tracking, satellite navigation systems, and optical odometry, the Kalman filter is considered crucial for a vehicle to operate autonomously.

Vehicular Ad-Hoc Networks (VANETs)

VANETs are a new subclass of mobile ad hoc networks that can spontaneously create a network of mobile devices/vehicles. Vehicle-to-vehicle (V2V) and vehicle-to-infrastructure (V2I) communication are possible with VANET.

The main objective of such technology is to increase road safety; For example, cars can interact with each other and the network to transmit crucial information in dangerous situations like accidents and traffic jams.

The following are the main components of VANET technology:

- OBU (on-board unit): A GPS-based tracking system in each vehicle allows them to interact with each other and with road units (RSU). The OBU has various electronic components, including a resource command processor (RCP), sensor devices, and user interfaces. , to obtain essential information. Its main purpose is to use a wireless network to communicate between multiple RSUs and OBUs.
- Roadside Unit (RSU): RSUs are fixed computing units placed at precise points on streets, parking lots, and intersections. Its main objective is to link autonomous vehicles to the infrastructure and help with vehicle location. Additionally, it can link a vehicle to other RSUs using various network topologies. In addition, they have been powered by environmental energy sources, including solar power.
- Trusted Authority (TA): This body controls every step of the VANET process, ensuring that only legitimate RSUs and vehicle OBUs can register and interact. By confirming the OBU ID and

authenticating the vehicle, it provides security. In addition, it finds harmful communications and strange behavior.

VANETs are used for vehicular communication, which includes V2V, V2I, and V2X communication.

Vehicle 2 Vehicle Communication

The ability of cars to talk to each other and exchange crucial information about traffic congestion, accidents, and speed restrictions is known as inter-vehicle communication (IVC).

V2V communication can create the network by joining several nodes (Vehicles) using a mesh topology, either partial or complete.

They are classified as single-hop (SIVC) or multi-hop (MIVC) systems depending on how many hops are used for inter-vehicle communication.

While MIVC can be used for long-range communications such as traffic control, SIVC can be used for short-range applications such as lane merging, ACC, etc.

Numerous benefits, including BSD, FCWS, Automated Emergency Braking (AEB), and LDWS, are offered through V2V communication.

Vehicle 2 Infrastructure Communication

Cars can communicate with RSU through a process known as road-to-vehicle communication (RVC). Helps detect parking meters, cameras, lane markers, and traffic signs.

Ad hoc, wireless and bidirectional connection between cars and infrastructure.

Infrastructure data is used for traffic management and monitoring. They adjust various speed parameters that allow cars to maximize fuel economy and manage traffic flow.

The RVC system can be separated into dispersed RVC (SRVC) and infrastructure-based ubiquitous RVC (URVC).

The SRVC system only offers communication services at access points, such as locating open parking spaces or gas stations. In contrast, the URVC system offers coverage along the entire route, even at high speeds.

To ensure network coverage, the URVC system requires a large investment.

Vehicle 2 All Communication

The car can connect with other entities through V2X, including pedestrians, objects on the road, devices, and Grid (V2P, V2R, and V2D) (V2G).

This communication prevents drivers from hitting pedestrians, bicyclists, and motorcyclists at risk.

The Pedestrian Collision Warning (PCW) system can warn the driver of a passenger on the road ahead of a catastrophic collision thanks to V2X communication.

The PCW can use the smartphone's Bluetooth or Near Field Communication (NFC) to send important messages to pedestrians.

Push Notification System Design

Goal

Develop a notification service that can efficiently distribute product-to-user messages through a variety of channels

Requirements :

- Send API – Publish an authorized endpoint so that any back-end and microservice can start sending notifications.
- Supported Channels – Supports delivery of alerts to any channel that publishes an API, such as email, text, and push.
- User Preferences: Allows users to select their user preferences for each channel and notification.
- Downstream Service Compliance Limits: Prevent your email or SMS service from being limited or stopped.
- Scalable: Allows (theoretically) infinite horizontal scaling.

High-Level Architecture

Let's say your code is supposed to notify someone:

- Your code invokes the POST /send endpoint. For each available channel, the request includes the recipient's user ID, the type of notification, and its content.
- The /send endpoint uses the OAuth2 client credential stream to authenticate the request.

- The user's notification options are then requested from the database. Preferences show whether or not the user is subscribed to a certain channel and notification.
- The database will read the users' characteristics, such as email addresses and phone numbers.
- This endpoint will create a message object that includes the characteristics of the user, channels, and channel-specific content. However, it will not include disabled channels. The message is then sent to a distribution service.
- Incoming messages are distributed to job queues through the fanout service. However, there is filtering to drop work queues for channels not specified in the message.
- Each channel has a processor and a work queue. The processor takes the task and then requests the appropriate service, such as a transactional email or SMS service.

Main Elements Of Architecture

POST/Sent

You may have noticed that only the user ID and neither the email address nor the phone number are included in the request to this endpoint. This allows notification services to remain anonymous to their users.

- To ensure scalability, the endpoint is placed behind a load balancer.
- Your typical user-facing authentication does not provide endpoint protection.
- You must use a different authentication method known as OAuth2 client credential flow for server-to-server communication since the service sending the request is the software itself.

Your app will provide notifications in many different places. You can use the push function almost anywhere, such as from a new code base or your build workflow, by deploying it as an endpoint behind a load balancer, ensuring that it is independently scalable.

PUT/User Preferences

Use a key/value pair or a NoSQL database that is extremely scalable. Format the records as follows: KEY: Sample User ID: Sample Notification ID, VALUE: ["email," "status: true," "SMS," "status: false," channel: "mail email," "email," status: true

If "false" values exist in the registers, the streaming endpoint will exclude the corresponding channel from the message delivered to the fanout. If there is no record for a channel, the user has not expressly indicated their preferences. You must accept default in this scenario.

Users can modify the data in the user preferences database using their user interface and a regular endpoint protected by their standard authentication procedures.

Users will get irritated and be forced to designate your alerts as spam or silence them if you don't give them the option to change their notification preferences. As a result, your user experience will be further impaired, and email or SMS-sending services may suspend your account.

Hand Fan

Fanout copies a message and distributes it to different locations. They are affordable and highly scalable. Use SNS on AWS. Use Pub/Sub on Azure and topics and subscriptions on Google Cloud Platform.

To avoid sending useless messages to work queues of excluded channels, you can configure filtering between the distribution and work queues. For example, in AWS SNS, you can specify that the email job queue should only receive the deployment message if it has the value "email" in the "channels" field.

Even if you could create code to send the same message to the required work queues, fanout is more efficient and requires less coding. Fanout also offers the convenience of adding and removing queues, allowing you to expand and rearrange your channels.

Job Processing

Messages are stored in queues pending processing by their job processors. They are also affordable and highly scalable. Job processors are pieces of code that process messages from job queues. Depending on the volume of messages in the queue, they can scale.

The job processor must make an API call to the appropriate provider to deliver the notice in our scenario via a transactional email service.

Most email, SMS, and similar delivery providers have strict requirements for the number and caliber of messages you send. Also, you want to examine these and establish the proper procedures thoroughly. Here is our advice on how to avoid getting fired from AWS SES.

You can define a maximum number of job processors to avoid exceeding delivery service rate limits.

Chapter 7: Essentials To Pass The Interview Successfully

As the name implies, the systems design interview aims to test the candidate's knowledge of the subject. But some things distinguish such an interview from a telephone conversation or programming assignments. In this case, the solution developed during the conversation will be only a "side effect," according to Palantir interviewers; the interview process is much more important.

In other words, communication is extremely important at this stage.

In modern companies, especially start-ups, which Palantir still is, engineers are rarely given tasks that are completely disassembled into the most detailed specifications. Instead, they are faced with the need to solve problems that it is not even immediately clear how to approach. And in the course of working on such tasks, it is extremely important that members of the engineering team can understand each other and move in the same direction. This means that the importance of effective communication is increasing exponentially.

At Palantir, interviewers usually ask the applicant to design a system that does a specific job. Everything seems not so complicated, but this impression is deceptive - the problems proposed for solving can be extremely broad and have more than one possible solution. Such tasks aim to understand how far the applicant can move in the allotted time (usually no more than 45 minutes).

The applicant must direct the conversation. It is necessary to find out all aspects of the task - to share with the interviewer the ideas that come to mind, to demonstrate your vision with the help of graphs and diagrams, to ask questions. What are the restrictions? Which of the input data should the system process? The search for solutions should begin only after a complete understanding of the problem. It is important to remember that a problem taken from real life cannot have the only correct solution.

What Topics To Pay Attention To When Preparing

Since the applicant will have to work with complex systems, he must be able to solve many diverse problems. For example, he should be able to speak on topics such as:

- Parallelism in programming (understanding of threads, locks, ability to "parallelize" algorithms, understanding of sequence);
- Networks (knowledge of the features of the IPC and TCP / IP network protocols, the difference between network bandwidth and its delay);
- Abstractions (understanding how the operating system, file system, and databases work. Understanding the different levels of caching in modern operating systems);
- Real performance (assessment of the speed of the task on the computer, the performance of the hard disk, SSD, RAM, or network);
- Preliminary calculation (the ability to quickly make small calculations on paper will help narrow down the range of possible solutions and sketch out prototypes before writing code);
- Fault tolerance (does the candidate see possible shortcomings in the system's functioning, does he understand how it will behave in case of problems with the network).

It is important to realize that representatives of IT companies do not expect a thorough description of all these working moments but appreciate their understanding.

The Most Effective Preparation Methods

Just as a basketball player must complete hundreds of sports exercises before he succeeds, an engineer, especially if he is not already very experienced, must write a lot of code and practice designing complex systems more than once. Here are the types of activities that will contribute to the professional growth of a novice specialist:

- Constant problem-solving. It's helpful to ask a fellow developer to share a few working cases or to think of a couple of common design problems to practice finding the best solution to possible problems.
- Working on a real system. Success can also be achieved by perceiving training tasks as something more important than part of the academic experience. It is important to analyze the architecture of each system that you have to work on and study other people's "real" projects.
- Checking the found solutions. If you write down on paper all the approximate calculations made during your work and then check

them with small tests, you can track typical errors in your reasoning.

- Exploring the performance of open source systems. Observing the implementation of someone else's code will help you understand how to store and compact data more efficiently.
- Analysis of the principles of operation of databases and operating systems. This is not only a "working" tool but also a source of non-standard professional solutions for an observant developer. Understanding the functioning of databases and operating systems will greatly simplify the work of an engineer because the same principles of functioning can become the basis for many other complex systems.

During the interview: calmness and creativity

A systems engineering interview seems daunting to many engineers, but it's a great opportunity to get creative by discussing projects that don't exist yet.

Suppose the applicant correctly understood the test item, considered the interviewer's comments, and demonstrated the ability to work in a team, discussing ideas. In that case, this practically guarantees that there will be no serious problems.

4 tips to Hack Your Next Systems Design Interview

The systems design interview is an open conversation. You are expected to lead it. To help solidly. Tagged "beginners," architecture, microservices, java.

The system design interview is an open conversation. You are expected to lead it.

To help reinforce this process, you can use the following steps to guide the discussion.

1. Describe use cases, limitations, and assumptions

Determine the scope and gather requirements of the problem. Ask questions to clarify use cases and limitations. Discuss the following assumptions:

- Who is the user?
- How are they will use it?
- How many users?

- What does the system required to do?
- What are the inputs and outputs?
- How much data do we expect to process?
- How many requests per second are expected?
- What is the expected ratio of reads and writes?

2. Create a high-level design

Outline the high-level design with all the important components.

- Draw the main components and connections
- Justify your ideas

3. Basic design components

Dive into the details for each major component. For example, if you were asked to create an Instagram-like website, discuss the details for each module in detail:

Example:

User authentication and authorization module

- Login/Registration flows.
- How will the user be authenticated when they log in and try to access your application?
- Database Schema
- What is your choice of the database? (SQL or NoSQL)
- API and Object Oriented Design

Timeline Module

- How a user's timeline will be displayed based on their followers.
- Database Schema
- What is your choice of the database? (SQL or NoSQL)
- API and Object Oriented Design

Always prioritize completing the high-level design of end-to-end user flows for a given problem statement.

4. Scale your design

Identify and bottle-eliminate necks, taking into account existing restrictions. For instance, do you need the following to solve scalability issues?

- load balancer
- Horizontal and vertical scaling
- caching
- Database segmentation

Discuss potential solutions and trade-offs. Eliminate bottlenecks, if any.

Most Common System Design Questions

- Develop a URL shortening service like bit.ly
- Create a social network like Facebook/Twitter/Instagram.
- Develop a taxi booking system similar to Uber.
- Create a web crawler.
- Create a video streaming service like Youtube.
- Develop a Quora/Reddit-like system.
- Develop a ticket booking system like Ticketmaster

Chapter 8: URL Shortening Service

Designing a URL shortener service is the most frequently asked question in the system design round of interviews. You will need to state your approach to designing this service within a limited time frame (45 minutes or less). Many candidates fear this question more than the coding round because they have no idea what topics and trade-offs they should cover within this limited period. First, remember that the system design round is extremely open, and there is no standard answer. You will have a different discussion with interviewers even for the same question.

You should design this web service where if a user provides a long URL, the service revenues a short URL, and if the user provides a short URL, it returns the original long URL. For example, shortening the given URL via TinyURL:

https://www.expertdesigner.org/get-your-dream-job-with-amazon-sde-test-series/?ref=leftbar-rightbar

We get the result shown below.

https://tinyurl.com/y7vg2xjl

Many candidates might think that designing this service is not difficult. When a user gives a long URL, convert it to a short URL and update the database and when the user accesses the short URL, look up the short URL in the database, get the long URL, and redirect the users to the original URL.

Don't immediately launch into technical details when you're asked this question in your interviews. Most candidates make mistakes here and immediately start listing off some tools, databases, and frameworks.

The following are the requirements:

1.   Requirement

Before jumping into the solution, always clarify any assumptions you're making at the start of the interview. Ask questions to identify the scope. This will clear the doubt, and you will know the specific details that the interviewer wants to consider in this service.

- The service should generate a shorter, more unique alias given a long URL.
- The service will redirect to the original link when the user accesses a short link.
- Links will expire after a standard predetermined period.

- The system must have high availability. This is very important to remember because if the service goes down, all URL redirection will start to fail.
- Shortened links shouldn't be predictable.

Let's start by making some assumptions about traffic (for scalability) and URL length.

2. Traffic

Let's assume that our service has 30 million new URL shorteners per month. Suppose we store each URL shortening request (and the associated shortened link) for 5 years. During this period, the service will generate about 1.8 B records.

30 million * 5 years * 12 months = 1.8B

3. URL length

Let's use 7 characters to create a short URL. These characters consist of a combination of 62 characters [AZ, az, 0-9], something like http://ad.com/abXdef2.

4. Data Capacity Modeling

Analyze the data capacity model to estimate system storage. We need to understand the amount of data we will have to insert into our system. Consider the different columns or attributes stored in our database and calculate the data storage for five years. Let's make the assumption:

- Consider an average long URL size of 2KB or 2048 characters.
- Short URL Size: 17 bytes for 17 characters
- Created at 7 bytes
- expiration_length_in_minutes -7 bytes

The above calculation will give 2,031 KB per shortened URL entry in the database. If we calculate the total storage, for 30M active users, the total size is = 30000000 * 2031 = 60780000 KB = 60.78 GB per month. In a year of 0.7284 TB and 5 years, 3,642 TB of data.

We need to consider the reads and writes that will occur to our system for this amount of data. This will decide what type of database (RDBMS or NoSQL) we need to use.

5. URL shortening logic (encoding)

To convert a long URL to a unique short URL, we can use some hash techniques like Base62 or MD5. We will discuss both approaches.

Base62 encoding: The Base62 encoder permits us to use the combination of characters and numbers that contains AZ, az, 0–9 in total (26 + 26 + 10 = 62). So for a short URL of 7 characters, we can serve $62^7 \sim= 3.5$ trillion URLs, which is enough compared to base10 (base10 only contains numbers from 0 to 9, so you will get only 10 million combinations). If we use base62, assuming the service generates 1,000 tiny URLs per second, it will take 110 years to exhaust this combination of 3.5 trillion. We can create a random number for the given long URL and change it to base62 by using the hash as a short URL ID.

def to_base_62(deci):

    s = '012345689abcdefghijklmnopqrstuvwxyzABCDEFGHIJKLMNOPQRSTUVXYZ'

    HashONE_str = ''

    while deci > 0:

        HashONE_str= s[deci % 62] + Hash_str

        deci /= 62

    return HashONE_str

print to_base_62(999)

MD5 encoding: MD5 also gives base62 as output, but MD5 hash gives a long output of more than 7 characters. The MD5 hash produces an output that is 128 bits long, so out of 128 bits, we'll need 43 bits to generate a small 7-character URL. MD5 can create many collisions. We may get a similar unique id for the short URL for two or many long URL entries, which could cause data corruption.

6. Database

We can use RDBMS with ACID properties, but one might face scalability problems using relational databases. Now, assuming you can use sharding and solve the scalability problem in RDBMS will increase the system's complexity. There are 30 million active users, so there will be conversions, many redirects, and the resolution of short URLs. Reading and writing will be heavy for these 30 million users, so scaling the RDBMS using shards will increase design complexity when we want to have our system distributed. It would help if you used consistent hashing to balance traffic and database queries in the case of RDBMS, and that is a complicated process. So to handle this huge amount of traffic on our system,

Now let's talk about NoSQL!

NoSQL can easily handle 30 million active users and is easy to scale.

Techniques for generating and storing TinyURL

Technique 1:

Let's discuss mapping a long URL to a short URL in our database. Suppose we create the Tiny URL using base62 encoding; then, we must do the steps below.

- The tiny URL must be unique, so first check for the existence of this tiny URL in the database (by doing get(tiny) on DB). If it's already there for another long URL, generate a new short URL.
- If short URL is not present in DB, put longURL and TinyURL in DB(put(TinyURL, longURL)).

This technique works great with one server, but if there are multiple servers, this technique will create a race condition. When multiple servers work together, there will be a chance that they can all generate the same unique ID or the same small URL for different long URLs. After checking the database, it is allowed to insert the same small URLs simultaneously (the same for different long URLs) in the database, which can corrupt the data.

Technique 2 (MD5 approach)

- Encode a long URL using the MD5 approach and take the first 7 characters to create TinyURL.
- The first 7 characters can be similar for different long URLs, so check the database (as discussed in technique 1) to verify that TinyURL hasn't already been used.
- Advantages: This approach saves some database space, but how? If two users want to generate a small URL for the same long URL, the first technique will generate two random numbers and requires two rows in the database. Still, in the second technique, both longer URLs will have the same MD5, so you have the same first 43 bits, which means we'll get some deduplication and save some space as we only require to store one row rather than two rows.

MD5 hoards a few spaces in the database for similar URLs, but for two long and different URLs, we will face the same problem we discussed in technique 1. We can use putIfAbsent, but NoSQL does not support this function. Let's move on to the third technique to solve this problem.

Chapter 9: General Principles For Passing An Interview On The Design Of IT Systems

You have just been invited to this coveted interview at your dream company. Your hiring coordinator sent you a schedule for the day. At first glance, everything is pretty good, but then you catch your eye on the interview item for IT systems design.

Many people are afraid of this kind of interview. Questions on them can be vague and too general, for example: "Design a well-known product X." The applicant's lack of enthusiasm is understandable. After all, who can design a popular product with hundreds, if not thousands, of engineers working on it in an hour?

The positive news is that no one expects this from you. Real systems have extremely complex architectures. For example, Google search only looks simple; the amount of technology behind this simplicity is truly amazing. But if no one expects you to be able to design a real system in an hour, then what is the use of this interview?

An IT systems design interview simulates a real-life process in which a pair of colleagues work together on some common, not entirely clear task and find a suitable solution. The problem is general, and there is no ideal solution. It is not so much the architecture that you propose that is important but the design process itself. This allows you to demonstrate your skills as an engineer, justify the choice of certain architectural solutions and constructively answer the questions that have arisen.

Let's put ourselves in the place of an interviewer - a person who asks questions and try to understand what he thinks about when he enters the conference room and meets you. Its main task is to assess your abilities correctly. The worst outcome for him will be a poorly conducted interview or lack of information that will not allow you to give a final assessment. What is the interviewer trying to discover during an IT systems design interview? Each IT systems design interview is unique.

Many believe this type of interview comes down to the applicant's technical design skills. But this is just a small part of it. An effective interview signals the applicant's ability to work collaboratively, withstand pressure, and deal constructively with vague tasks. Another key skill that many interviewers pay particular attention to is the ability to ask the right questions.

A good interviewer also looks for negative signs. Overly complicated architectural solutions are a real disease of many engineers who admire the purity of the result and are unwilling to compromise. They are often unaware of the costs of overcomplicated systems, and this ignorance is costly for many companies. This tendency is not worth demonstrating. Among other undesirable qualities, narrow-mindedness, stubbornness, etc., can be distinguished.

This chapter will discuss useful tips and offer a simple and effective approach to solving problems in an IT system design interview.

A Successful IT Design Interview in 4 Steps

A good problem should be general and not have one universal solution. But all interviews have common steps.

Step 1: understand the problem and determine the scope of the solution

- Why did the tiger growl?

In the back row, someone willingly raised their hand.

— Jimmy? The teacher nodded.

Because he's HUNGRY.

Great, Jimmy. Let's see how the development of a common architecture takes place using the example of a news feed.

In his class, Jimmy was always the first to answer questions. Whenever a teacher asks something, there will always be a child in the class who will gladly risk raising his hand, even if he does not have an answer. In our case, it's Jimmy.

Jimmy is excellent. He prides himself on his ability to answer all questions quickly. In exams, he usually turns in his paper before everyone else. He is the first on the list of those the teacher sends to the Olympiads.

DON'T BE like Jimmy.

Quick responses without thinking in an IT systems design interview will not give you extra points. Solving a problem without a deep understanding of its requirements is bad since such an interview is not a quiz. There is simply no right answer.

Therefore, do not rush to offer a solution. Hold up. Think carefully and ask questions to clarify requirements and assumptions. This is extremely important.

We engineers love complex problems and are in a hurry to come up with ready-made solutions, but this approach most likely will not lead to the design of the desired systems. One of the most important skills of any engineer is asking the right questions, making the right assumptions, and gathering all the information needed to build a system. So don't be afraid to ask.

Upon hearing the question, the interviewer will answer directly or ask you to come up with your assumptions. Writing down your thoughts on a board or paper is better in the second case. You will need them later. Candidate: "Is this a mobile or web application? Or both?" Interviewer: "Both." Candidate: "What are the most important features this product should have?" Interviewer: "The ability to publish articles and your friends' news feeds to see." Candidate: "Is the feed sorted chronologically or in some special order? Special order means that each article is assigned a certain weight. For example, the articles of your close friends are more important than those published in the group.

What should you ask? Try to clarify the architecture requirements. Here is a list of questions to start with:

— What opportunities will we implement?

How many users does our product have?

- How soon is the capacity increase expected? What scale is planned in 3 months, half a year, or a year?

— What does the technology stack of the company look like? What existing services can be applied to simplify the architecture?

Example

If you are asked to design a news feed, you should clarify its requirements. Your conversation with the interviewer might look like this:

Interviewer: "To keep things simple, let's assume the tape is sorted in reverse chronological order."

Candidate: "How many friends can a user have?"

Interviewer: "5000".

Candidate: "How much traffic?"

Interviewer: "10 million daily active users (DAU)".

Candidate: "Can the feed contain images, video files, and text?"

Interviewer: "There can be media files in the feed, including images and videos."

The above are some of the questions you can ask your interviewer. It is important to define the requirements and clarify ambiguous points.

Step 2: offer a common solution and get an agreement

At this stage, we are trying to find a common solution and agree with the interviewer. It is highly desirable to establish joint work during this process.

- Propose an initial architecture plan. Ask for the interviewer's opinion. Treat him like a member of your team with whom you work together. Good interviewers often like to talk and participate in problem-solving.
- Draw flowcharts on a whiteboard or paper with key components such as clients (mobile/browser), APIs, web servers, data stores, caches, CDNs, message queues, etc.
- Perform approximate calculations to see if your solution fits the scale of the problem. Think loud. Before counting anything, talk to the interviewer.

Go through a few specific use cases, if possible. This will help you form a common architecture and most likely discover edge cases you haven't thought of yet.

Should I designate API endpoints and database schema at this point? It depends on the task. If you're being asked to design something big, like Google search, it's best not to go that deep. These aspects can be indicated if we discuss the server part of a multiplayer poker game. Chat with the interviewer.

Example:

At a high level, the architecture is divided into two streams: publishing articles and compiling a news feed.

- Posts in the feed. When a user publishes a post, the relevant information is written to the cache or database, and the post appears in his friends' news feeds.
- Compilation of the news feed. The news feed is formed by grouping your friends' posts in reverse chronological order.

Step 3: Deep Dive into Design

At this point, you and the interviewer have achieved the following goals:

- agreed on the overall requirements and future scope;
- drafted an approximate architecture diagram;
- learned the opinion of the interviewer about your overall decision;
- got some basic idea of what areas to focus on in detailed design (based on what the interviewer answered).

Working with the interviewer, you should identify the components of the architecture and prioritize them. It is worth emphasizing that all interviews are conducted differently. Sometimes you may be given to understand that it is desirable to focus on the overall architecture. Occasionally, suppose the candidate is applying for a major position. In that case, the discussion may touch on the performance characteristics of the system, likely focusing on bottlenecks and an estimate of the resources required.

In most cases, the candidate is asked to delve into the details of some system components. If you're designing a service to shorten URLs, you'll be particularly interested in a hash function that turns a long address into a short one. In the messaging system, two interesting aspects are latency reduction and support for online/offline statuses.

The rational use of time plays a key role. It's easy to get hung up on unimportant details that don't appreciate your ability. You must show the interviewer what he wants to know about you. Try not to delve into unnecessary details. For example, it's best not to get into a detailed discussion of the EdgeRank algorithm that Facebook uses to weight posts in its feed. It takes valuable time and doesn't demonstrate your ability to design scalable systems.

Example:

So we've discussed the general architecture of the news feed, and the interviewer approved of your decision. We will now explore the two most important use cases.

- Publication of posts.
- Issuance of a news feed.

Step 4: Debriefing

At the final stage, you may be asked a few follow-up questions or invited to discuss other aspects of your choice. Here are some tips to guide you.

The interviewer may ask you to identify bottlenecks in the system and discuss potential improvements. Never claim that your solution is perfect. You can always improve something.

- It might be worth reviewing your architecture, especially if you have proposed several solutions. This will allow the interviewer to refresh his memory, which can come in handy after a long interview.
- It will be interesting to talk about emergencies, such as server breakdowns, network breaks, etc.
- It is worth touching on operational issues. How do you track metrics and error logs? How is the system rolled out?
- Carrying out the next scaling stage is also a very interesting topic. For example, if your current architecture supports 1 million users, what changes would you need to make to increase that number to 10 million?

If there is still time, suggest further improvements.

Recommended:

- Always clarify. Don't rely on your assumptions to be correct.
- Decide on requirements.

There is no right or best answer. A young startup and a well-known company with millions of users have different architectures that solve different problems. Make sure you understand the requirements.

- Share your thoughts with the interviewer. Chat with him.
- If possible, offer different approaches.

After agreeing on the overall architecture with the interviewer, discuss each component in detail. Start designing with the most important components.

- Offer different ideas. A good interviewer treats the candidate like a member of their team.
- Never give up.

Not recommended:

- Do not come to the interview without preparing for typical questions.
- Don't start working on a solution until you've clarified the requirements and assumptions.
- Do not devote too much time to any one component at once. Propose a general architecture, and then dive into the details.

If you're having trouble, don't hesitate to ask for help.

"Again, don't shut yourself up. Don't talk silently.

Don't think the interview is over once you've made your decision. The interviewer decides whether to continue or not. Constantly ask for his opinion.

Time allotted for each step

The questions in an IT system design interview are usually very general, and 45 minutes or an hour is not enough to discuss the entire architecture. It is very important to use your time wisely. How many minutes should be allocated for each step? The following are very rough guidelines for breaking up a 45-minute interview. Please keep in mind that these are only rough estimates: the time distribution depends on the scope of the task and the requirements that the interviewer voiced.

Step 1. Understand the problem and set the scope: 3-10 minutes.

Step 2: Propose a common solution and get approval: in 10-15 minutes.

Step 3: Detailed Design: 10-25 minutes.

Step 4 Debriefing: 3-5 minutes.

Chapter 10: System Design Interview Questions

When speaking with a potential employer, how you present your experience can help show that you are a competent candidate for the position.

You can prepare for your job interview by learning design basics and thinking about how you will respond to inquiries about them. We'll review some typical systems design interview questions and answers in this chapter to help you prepare for your next interview.

The systems designer interview is an opportunity to discuss your experience and abilities and showcase your skills in building complex systems. You can prepare for an interview by learning the basic design principles and preparing answers to possible questions about them. This chapter covers common system design interview questions and answers to help you prepare.

Systems Design Interview Questions and Answers

System design questions are usually ambiguous to allow you to demonstrate your expertise. You can ask questions before answering to help narrow down the field, give you direction, and clarify any expectations.

Here are common questions you might be asked during a system design interview:

1. How would you design a tinyURL?

TinyURL is a URL service that allows users to enter a long URL and then return a shorter, unique URL. The hiring manager may ask for this to allow you to showcase your strong foundations in design. You can focus on other basics not listed in the sample answer, such as how you create a unique ID for each URL, handle redirects, and remove expired URLs.

Example: "When I was working on a public instant messaging site, I was tasked with building a simple system where each message was limited to 140 characters. It also required shortening the URLs by about 30 characters. This system of tiny URLs is also useful when entering hyperlinks in email messages. TinyURL is a great example of a hashtag table. Using this basic 16-bit hash table, I optimized usability and satisfied the system's needs."

2. How would you design a search engine?

Sometimes search engines are needed in a particular department of a company to find an item or important information about employees systematically. Hiring administrators want to see that you can tailor the design to the company's needs. You can detail part of the overall architecture and explain it with the framework below. You may also consider discussing other important issues, such as website front-end performance, testing engine improvements, and integrating previous search data and indexing trends.

Example: "Before I moved here, I was working on a project like this. The search engine I had to create had to work with keyword searches. I started by creating an indexer, a piece of software crawling and returning the results as a data structure. The crawler collected links to web pages and grouped them or uploaded them into sets. The indexer was then run as part of the reduction job to extract the elements. For every website, the number of links was counted. And analyzed for presentation. I set the scan for H1 and H2, not H3. I then checked outgoing links to avoid spammers. Finally, I checked the maintenance results to ensure the design runs at optimal throughput and relevancy."

3. How do you design a crawler, and when should you use it?

A search robot is a program designed to visit other sites and read their information. This information is then used to create entries for the search engine index. It is commonly referred to as a "bot" or "spider." Don't forget to show in your explanation that you know the ins and outs of web crawling.

Example: "Even though scanning the web is challenging, I was able to create one for a previous project. The scanner collects data from a specific sector, in this case, the fashion industry. I needed to integrate a URL manager, a server whose job is to propagate the start URL to multiple servers. The crawl manager then passes the URL to the bots using the developed messaging queue. The spider, the backbone of any web crawler, extracts data from a web page and downloads it to my file system. Extract, Transform, and Load (ETL), then cleaned up the content and reformatted it to store it in the database. Thus, I was able to scan the Internet in search of and organize the necessary information. "

4. How do you design the overall drive?

Hiring managers ask for this to learn the basics of the algorithm and backstory. Make sure you understand the purpose of the task. Knowing whether changes will be logged in real-time, whether locking will be necessary, and whether it should converge naturally will help you give a complete answer.

Example: "This system works with differential timing. It keeps two or more copies of the same document in sync with each other in real-time, consequently if a change is made to one version, the same change happens to all the others. Challenging task, but differential timing is scalable and fault-tolerant. Three common approaches are ownership, event passing, and three-way merging. The last time I had to do this was to support an internal document exchange for one of our clients. Collaborating in time, so a three-way merge was not a good option as changes are lost and cannot take effect as major conflicts are common. I used event passing to enable real-time collaboration since the lock or own approach would only allow the first to open the document to make any adjustments. This served our client well as his employees could work together even when they were away from the office or on different schedules."

5. What is required to design a garbage collection system?

Garbage collection ensures that the Java system works correctly and frees the programmer from having to do it manually. Hiring administrators are looking to see if you know how to properly design the inputs and outputs of various systems. The garbage collector makes the system memory efficient.

Example: "One of my recent clients needed a way to have more memory but had a problem with always having to go in and deal with freeing the memory. The essence of garbage collection is to make the system look like this, an infinite amount of memory. What happens is that the system reallocates memory. When the system runs slowly, the garbage collector kicks in and collects what is no longer in use. I set up their system so that it stays if an object is a reference or recursive. It then methodically goes through, marks everything that was not referenced, and clears only that. Using the mark and clear method with the void command helps to reassign and open memory that is no longer in use.

6. How do you develop a recommendation system?

Recommendation systems help clients and customers by offering alternatives and providing choices. Hiring managers ask this to see if you can create user-friendly and targeted systems.

Example: "One of my earliest and most loyal customers had a problem when his customers struggled to find options on their website. Their search had to be precise to find a product. I suggested implementing a referral system to help with clients. Satisfaction and possible sales. Using the best-known collaborative filtering approach, I developed a system to weave an informational tapestry to give our clients' customers suggestions based on user similarity. The system became more user-friendly and increased the number of customers by 10%. Sales for my client.

7. What Do You Understand By System Design?

The process of establishing system characteristics, including modules, architecture, components, interfaces, and data based on predetermined criteria, is known as system design.

It is the process of defining, creating, and designing systems to meet a company's or organization's specific goals and objectives.

8. State The Most Important Characteristics Of A System Designer.
- User interaction
- External API call
- offline processes

9. What Exactly Is The CAP Theorem?

According to the CAP (Coherence-Availability-Partition Tolerance) theorem, a distributed system cannot simultaneously guarantee C, A, and P. You can only deliver two of the three guarantees at most. Let's use a distributed database system to help us understand this.

- Consistency: This specifies that data should remain consistent after a database transaction completes. For example, all queries should return the same response after a database update.
- Availability: Databases must be available and responsive at all times.
- Partition Tolerance – The database system should continue functioning if communication becomes problematic.

10. What Do You Understand By Load Balancing?

Load balancing is efficiently dispersing incoming traffic among a set of back-end servers. These are known as server groups. Modern websites handle millions of customer inquiries and respond quickly and reliably. More servers will be needed to handle these demands.

In this case, it is critical to divide the request traffic efficiently between servers to avoid overloading them. The load balancer works like a traffic police officer, intercepting requests and routing them between available servers so that no server is overloaded, which could degrade application performance.

11. State The Difference Between Asynchronous Programming And Parallel Programming.

When you run something asynchronously, you don't need to wait for it to end before you can move on to something else. Parallelism refers to the simultaneous execution of many tasks.

Parallelism works effectively when you can split jobs into different parts of the job. Async and Callbacks are a means (tool or mechanism) to represent concurrency, a group of entities that could communicate and share resources.

12. State The Difference Between Horizontal And Vertical Scales.

Adding new computing equipment to a network that spreads processing and memory demand across a dispersed network of devices is called scaling out. New server instances are added to the current pool, and the traffic load is distributed efficiently across these devices.

Vertical scaling refers to expanding the resource capacity of a single computer by adding RAM, efficient CPUs, or migrating to a new machine with higher capacity. Server functionality can be increased without the need for programming changes.

13. What Exactly Do You Mean By System Latency, Throughput, And Availability?

Performance is an essential aspect of system design as it contributes to the speed and reliability of our services. The three most important performance measures are as follows:

- The time it takes to deliver a single message in milliseconds is called latency.
- The amount of data successfully transferred through a system in a given period is known as throughput.

14. What Are The Properties Of ACIDS?

- Atomicity: Ensures that database alterations are all or none.
- Consistency: The data values in the database are consistent.
- Isolation: Refers to the separation of two transactions.
- Durability: data is preserved even if the server fails.

15. What Exactly Is Fragmentation?

Sharding is dividing a huge set of logical data into many databases. It also refers to the horizontal division of data because it will be stored on multiple computers. As a result, a shared database can handle more queries than a single huge computer.

16. What Is CDN?

A content delivery network is a worldwide network of computers collaborating to deliver information from the Internet quickly. It enables fast delivery of elements such as HTML pages, JavaScript files, style sheets, images, and videos necessary to load content from the Internet.

17. Why Use CDN?

- Since static resources comprise around 80% of a website, adopting a CDN significantly reduces the strain on the origin server.
- Since there is less distance to travel, information will be provided faster to website owners who have visitors from many geographic areas.
- CDN users also benefit from the ability to scale up and down quickly in response to spikes in traffic.

18. What Is The Difference Between Fragmentation And Partition?

Database sharding – Database sharding divides a single data set into numerous databases to store it on different workstations. Larger data sets can be broken into smaller chunks and stored across multiple data nodes, increasing the system's total storage capacity.

Distributing data across many machines allows a shared database to handle more queries than a single system.

Database partitioning divides stored database objects (tables, indexes, and views) into separate parts. Large database objects are partitioned to increase controllability, performance, and availability.

In some cases, partitioning can improve speed when accessing partitioned data. Partitioning can reduce the index size and increase the chance of allocating the most needed indexes in memory by acting as a starting column in the indexes.

19. What Exactly Is Caching?

Caching is the technique of keeping copies of files in a temporary storage area known as a cache, which speeds up data access and reduces site latency. Only a certain amount of data can be stored in the cache.

As a result, it is critical to determine the most appropriate cache update techniques for your business objectives.

20. What Are CDN Edge Servers?

CDN servers that cache material purchased from your origin server or storage cluster are known as edge servers. Point of presence is often used to describe edge servers (POPs).

Edge Servers are physically placed in a POP. In that POP, many edge servers can cache the information.

The ability to serve sections of a website from multiple locations reduces the distance between the visitor and the web server, resulting in lower latency. CDN Edge Servers accomplish this precise goal.

21. What Are The Different Consistency Patterns For System Design?

According to the CAP theorem, each read request must retrieve the most recently written data. When many copies of data are accessible, synchronizing them so that clients receive continuously updated data becomes difficult. The following are the possible consistency patterns:

- Weak consistency: After a data write, the read request may or may not get the updated data. This level of stability is ideal for real-time applications such as VoIP, video chat, and multiplayer gaming.
- Eventual consistency: Reads will eventually see the most recent data within milliseconds after writing the data. In this case, the data is replicated asynchronously. DNS and email systems are examples of this. This works effectively on systems with high availability.
- Great consistency: Future readers will see the most recent data after data. In this case, the data is copied synchronously. This can be seen in RDBMS and file systems, which are suitable for data transfers.

22. What Do You Mean By Optimistic Locking?

Optimistic locking is a mechanism where you read a record, note a version number (alternative forms include dates, timestamps, or checksums/hashes), and verify that the version hasn't changed before writing it back.

When it writes the record back, it uses the version to filter the update to ensure it's atomic. (i.e., it hasn't changed between the time you check the version and when you write the record to disk) and update it all at once.

23. What Exactly Do You Mean By "Leader Election"?

In a distributed system with many servers contributing to application availability, there may be times when only one server is responsible for updating third-party APIs, as multiple servers can cause problems using the APIs.

This server is the main server, and the procedure for selecting it is known as the leader election. When the lead server fails in a distributed system, the servers must notice the failure and elect a new leader. This approach best suits applications with high availability and strong consistency using a consensus technique.

24. What Is Your Approach To Designing A URL Shortening Service Similar To TinyURL?

TinyURL transforms a long URL into a unique short URL. These technologies can also accept a short URL and return the full URL.

What are some of the crucial qualities?

- Make a URL that is shorter than the original.
- Keep the longer URL and replace it with the shorter one.
- Allow redirection on short URLs.
- Short URLs with custom names are supported.
- Handle multiple queries at once.

What are the most frequent problems?

- How is database storage tracked?
- What happens if the user load exceeds expectations?
- What if two people use the same custom URL?

Consider the following suggestions:

- Hashing is a notion that can be used to connect old and new URLs.
- REST API can be used to handle front-end communication and heavy load balancing.
- Multithreading is a notion that allows you to handle multiple requests at once.
- The original URLs are stored in NoSQL databases.

25. What Is Your Approach To Designing Twitter?

Requirements given:

- Sending tweets
- Following other users
- Tweet/news feed
- The system is scalable
- It charges quickly

- The system is reliable

You can start thinking about the design of your Twitter API once you have established the criteria. This is how it would appear:

To get started, we'll outline the key API endpoints. Here are some examples:

- send a tweet(message)
- follower(user ID)
- unfollow user (User ID)
- get fed(page)

The architecture that will enable these features can then be outlined. We can start with the user submitting a server request. We can install additional API servers behind a load balancer to help route larger traffic levels to meet the need for scalability. We'll need to add a database to store our tweets now.

It is important to remember that the API we provide must be scalable. To make this service scalable, we can have one of our API servers read from a separate cache for our newsfeed. In doing so, we should also use a feed provider to keep our feed cache up.

26. Create The Newsfeed System For Facebook

The Facebook newsfeed lets users see what's happening in their friends' circles, favorite Pages, and organizations they've followed.

What are some of the essential features?

- Create a newsfeed based on posts from other entities in the system that the user follows.
- Text, images, audio, and video can be used in Newsfeed posts.
- In real-time, add new content to the user's newsfeed.
- What are some of the most common problems?
- What if it takes a long time for the new post to appear in the feed?
- Can the algorithm handle a spike in user activity?
- Which posts should show first in the news feed?

Consider the following suggestions:

- Examine the fanning mechanism for distributing posts to followers.
- Examine how sharding can be used to handle large user loads efficiently.
- A user's power data should not be duplicated on multiple servers. Instead, sharding can be done based on user IDs.

27. What Is The BASE Property Of A System?

BASE features are ubiquitous in the NoSQL databases that have emerged recently. A BASE system does not provide consistency, according to the CAP theorem. This is an invented acronym that corresponds to the following property of a system of the CAP theorem:

- The term "basically available" means that the system will always be available.
- A soft state means that the system's state can vary over time, even if no input is provided. This is mainly due to the eventual consistency of the model.
- Since the system receives no input during that period, eventual consistency implies that the system will consequently become consistent over time.

28. What Is Load Balancing With IP Address Affinity Technique?

Another prominent method of load balancing is IP address affinity. The IP address of the client is connected to a server node in this method. A server node handles all requests for a client IP address.

This method is simple to implement as the IP address is always accessible in the HTTP request header, and no additional configuration is required. If your clients are likely to have cookies disabled, this load balancing may be advantageous.

29. What Exactly Are Cache Replacement Algorithms (Or Eviction Policy)?

Cache algorithms (cache replacement algorithms, cache replacement policies, or cache eviction policies) are optimization instructions or algorithms that a computer program or hardware-maintained structure can use to manage a cache. The cache of data stored on the computer.

Caching increases speed by storing recently used or frequently accessed data in memory regions that are faster or less expensive to access than traditional memory storage. Once the cache is full, the algorithm must decide which items to remove to make room for new ones.

30. What Exactly Do You Mean By Distributed Transaction?

A distributed transaction is any circumstance in which a single event causes the alteration of two or more different data sources that cannot be atomically committed.

It gets much more complicated in microservices as each service is a unit of work. More often than not, numerous services must collaborate for a business to succeed.

31. What Exactly Is Hunger?

When a thread cannot acquire regular access to shared resources, it is said to be starving. This occurs when "greedy" threads or higher "priority" threads make shared resources inaccessible for long periods.

Consider an object that provides a synchronized method that frequently returns late. If one thread repeatedly calls this method, it will often block other threads that require frequent synchronized access to the same object.

Conclusion

These are not universal principles, but I hope they serve as an example to help you evaluate your system design work.

" Designing a system is like a blueprint for action that will guide the rest of the team."

The art of system design lies in getting the scale right—providing enough information to represent the product accurately, but not so much that it becomes a 1:1 image of the product.

If you do everything right, you will have an invaluable document that will unite your team around a common task. This is a powerful tool that will help you navigate the difficulties that lie ahead of you.

A brainstorming session is all that is involved in the system design interview. We have addressed the most common system design interview questions in this book.

A comprehensive understanding of the method you are taking when creating a specific system is critical to passing a systems design interview.

References

https://github.com/checkcheckzz/system-design-interview

https://www.techinterviewhandbook.org/system-design/

https://blog.pragmaticengineer.com/preparing-for-the-systems-design-and-coding-interviews/

https://web.stanford.edu/class/archive/cs/cs110/cs110.1196/static/lectures/19-principles-of-system-design.pdf

https://www.tryexponent.com/courses/fundamentals-system-design/system-design-principles

https://durejatanmay.medium.com/system-design-principles-an-overview-1c886e16d51

https://cloud.google.com/architecture/framework/system-design/principles

https://www.geeksforgeeks.org/5-common-system-design-concepts-for-interview-preparation/

https://completedesigninterviewcourse.com/system-design-concepts-components/

https://www.interviewbit.com/courses/system-design/system-design-concepts/

https://towardsdatascience.com/the-complete-guide-to-the-system-design-interview-ba118f48bdfc

https://www.nasa.gov/seh/4-design-process

https://www.tutorialspoint.com/system_analysis_and_design/system_design.htm

https://www.educative.io/courses/grokking-the-system-design-interview/m2ygV4E81AR

https://medium.com/@sandeep4.verma/system-design-scalable-url-shortener-service-like-tinyurl-106f30f23a82

https://www.enjoyalgorithms.com/blog/design-a-url-shortening-service-like-tiny-url

https://www.interviewbit.com/system-design-interview-questions/

https://www.simplilearn.com/system-design-interview-questions-article

https://www.pramp.com/dev/uc-system-design?utm_source=quora&utm_medium=answer&utm_campaign=sd-def7ef

https://leetdesign.com/

Top 12 System Design Interview Questions with Answers (2022) | by Arslan Ahmad | Geek Culture | Aug 2022 | Medium

System Design Interviews: A Step-By-Step Guide (designgurus.org)

System Design Tutorial: 3 Must-Know Distributed Systems Concepts | by Arslan Ahmad | Geek Culture | Sep 2022 | Medium

How to prepare for the System Design Interview in 2022 (educative.io)

https://hackernoon.com/top-10-system-design-interview-questions-for-software-engineers-8561290f0444

Xu_-Alex-System-Design-Interview---An-Insider_s-Guide-_2020_-Byte-Code-LLC_-libgen.li.pdf

King_-Groks-System-Design-Interview-_-Mastering-Basic-Introduction-to-System-Analysis-and-Design-_20.pdf

Grokking%20the%20Advanced%20System%20Design%20Interview%20(2021,%20educative.io)%20-%20libgen.li.pdf

Made in the USA
Las Vegas, NV
30 December 2024

15602470R00063